D1631169

# A Season in New York, 1801

# A Season in New York 1801

LETTERS OF HARRIET
AND MARIA TRUMBULL
EDITED, WITH AN
INTRODUCTION BY

HELEN M. MORGAN

UNIVERSITY OF PITTSBURGH PRESS

Library of Congress Catalog Card Number 69–12333

*Manufactured in the United States of America*

*For Penny and Pam*

# PREFACE

THE letters of Harriet and Maria Trumbull are in the Sterling Memorial Library of Yale University, dispersed amidst other correspondence of the Silliman family in numerous chronologically arranged files. Had I first encountered them there in the course of absorbing the diverse subject matter with which they are mixed, I would probably have passed them by as mere girlish chatter. They first came to me, however, in the form of a transcript that Professor Norman Holmes Pearson had made before the collection was broken up. Reading the letters consecutively, I was struck by the fact that they illustrate in a remarkably compact space much about social history that scholars have had to learn gradually from a mountain of miscellaneous sources. They also contain revelations of their own about manners, morals, and the structure of society. I realized when I finished reading that two young girls had just given me a new understanding, feeling, and picture of what it was like to be alive in 1801 in New York.

The dispersal of the letters left small chance that they would ever again be read continuously, and without continuity the picture is invisible. Because I believe it will be of use to scholars and of interest to anyone who enjoys reading history, and because the sources of social history are slender compared to those of political history, and especially slender concerning the world of women, I have prepared the present edition of the New York letters of Harriet and Maria Trumbull. These are only a small part of the girls' letters that have survived, but the others were written at various times from various places and therefore lack continuity. All were apparently saved by Mrs. Trumbull and remained in Harriet's branch of the family until 1959 when Miss Maria Trumbull Dana gave them to Yale. The letters that Governor and Mrs. Trumbull wrote to the girls during their visit to New York are missing. I am indebted to Professor Pearson not only for a transcript of the letters but also for an index file of all names contained in them which he had made at a time when he contemplated editing the letters himself. Professor Pearson, Professor Julian Boyd, and my husband, Edmund S. Morgan, have given me valuable criticism. Mr. Gary Gore is gratefully acknowledged for his excellent drawing of the map of New York.

## *Editorial Note*

In transcribing the letters I have made the following changes to facilitate the printing and the reader's understanding.

1. Superscript abbreviations have either been expanded or modernized.

2. Where the letterwriter has indicated a new sentence by only a period or a capital letter, I have supplied the missing period or capital.

3. Occasionally, and only where the meaning was difficult to follow, I have indicated a sentence which the writer intended but did not so mark; or I have added (according to the stylistic preference of the writer) a clarifying comma (in Harriet's letters) or dash (in Maria's).

4. Words unintentionally repeated by the letterwriter (or repeated and then deleted) have been omitted.

5. Italicized words within brackets have been supplied by the editor and do not exist in the text.

6. Words within brackets but not italicized are part of the text but torn, obscured by sealing wax, or otherwise illegible so that they must remain conjectural. After uncertain conjectures I have added a question mark, and where conjecture was impossible the effacement has been described [i.e. *torn*].

7. All salutations and signatures have been rendered in capital letters, and complimentary closings have been made continuous with the body of the letters. The addressee and place of address have been incorporated into the headings rather than repeated in full for each letter. Those from the girls to their father were addressed:

His Excellency Governor Trumbull<br>
Hartford [*or Lebanon*]<br>
Connecticut

Daniel Wadsworth addressed his simply:

Governor Trumbull<br>
Hartford

The rest were directed to

Mrs. Jonathan Trumbull<br>
Lebanon [*or Hartford*]<br>
Connecticut

# CONTENTS


| | |
|---|---|
| Preface | vii |
| Introduction | 1 |
| Letters | 49 |
| Index | 179 |

# A Season in New York, 1801

*Jonathan Trumbull, Jr.*

*Mrs. Jonathan Trumbull, Jr.*

*Maria Trumbull*

*Harriet Trumbull*

---

*Jonathan Trumbull, Jr.*, by John Trumbull (Yale University Art Gallery). *Mrs. Jonathan Trumbull, Jr.*, by John Trumbull (Yale University Art Gallery, gift of Miss Maria Trumbull Dana). *Maria Trumbull* (Ink silhouette owned by Mrs. Philip H. English). *Harriet Trumbull* by Elkanah Tisdale (Yale University Art Gallery, gift of Miss Maria Trumbull Dana).

# INTRODUCTION

## *New York and Connecticut at the Opening of the Nineteenth Century*

On the first day of December, 1800, Harriet and Maria Trumbull of Lebanon, Connecticut arrived in New York City. Maria was a lively fifteen year old with an irrepressible sense of humor, eager for adventure, ready to try anything, and inclined to regard her elder sister as "old propriety." Harriet, timid, anxious, and indeed more strait-laced, had just reached her seventeenth birthday in September and was trying hard to appear grown up. The girls had come to New York to live for six months in the family of Lady Kitty Duer, who was a complete stranger to them.

The letters that Harriet and Maria wrote home from New York may be enjoyed for themselves simply as a candid account of two teen-age country girls on their first visit to a big city. The letters may also be read as history, for they reveal details of social life and evoke a social atmosphere that no historian could convey with equal authenticity. There is, however, another kind of significance involved but one that is less easy to grasp. Behind the everyday experiences of Harriet and Maria in the year 1801 lay not simply their years of country living but the fact that they grew up in the particular state of Connecticut at a particular time, and that the New York where they found themselves was not just a city but a particular city, one that had not been so totally isolated from rural Connecticut as one might suppose from that Puritan colony's previous history. Embedded in the Trumbull girls' casual reports of people and events and comings and goings between Connecticut and New York is evidence that Connecticut, during Harriet and Maria's short life, had established a surprising number of economic and social connections with the metropolis. Old letters often contain more than meets the eye, hints, suggestions, echoes of relationships and ideas about society that the writer took for granted or may not even have been aware of and that the modern reader may not perceive unless he has more information than the letters themselves contain. The following essay offers information about New York and Connecticut that helps to explain the letterwriters' reactions to people and events. And, for readers who enjoy detecting implications and overtones, the essay offers a few clues (others are in footnotes to the letters) that have come to light in the editor's efforts to identify the people whom the girls met and the web of relationships that bound them all together. Those who prefer simply to spend an hour with two charming teen-agers in early New York should proceed at once to the letters.

## *The Social Scene*

It was not unusual in the eighteenth century for girls and boys of all ages to be shipped from home—as were Harriet and Maria Trumbull—and committed to the care of slight acquaintances or complete strangers. For some it was a matter of necessity: because their own parents had not the means to support or educate them, they were placed in another family to earn their keep as helpers and to receive instruction in the arts of housekeeping, farming, storekeeping, or trade. Such youngsters were part of the Trumbull household and are mentioned in these letters. But parents who had no financial need to send their sons and daughters away often did so; and often, during the absence of their own children, they took in someone else's. Even wealthy children had to endure the experience of separation by long visits with families of appropriate social standing.

This widespread uprooting of the young seems to have been prompted in part by a belief that natural affection blinded parents to the faults of their offspring and that a child would benefit from an environment in which discipline and criticism were not blunted by love. Separation from the family might also cultivate a child's emotional self-sufficiency and counteract unduly strong ties to mother and father. Moreover no parent of a teen-age daughter could overlook the fact that out-of-town visiting would enlarge her acquaintance with eligible bachelors. But the benefits of visiting were not all to the visitor. A new personality in the house brought outside stimulation and a break in social monotony, especially welcome wherever life was circumscribed by the narrow limits of a small town or an isolated farm. For one reason or another, ever since the American colonies were founded, children had done some of their growing up under the roofs of strangers, friends, and relatives.[1]

Before the War for Independence, few Connecticut families knew anyone in New York to whom they could or would entrust their children; the Puritan colony had from the beginning been culturally oriented toward the rest of New England and was distrustful of its unpuritan western neighbor. The achievement of independence did not erase Connecticut's distrust (as is evident in these letters), but it

1. Edmund S. Morgan, *The Puritan Family* (New York, 1966), pp. 65–86; *Virginians at Home* (Williamsburg, 1952), pp. 5–28, 83.

did bring about political, social, and economic changes that made visiting New York both feasible and desirable—especially for upper-class teen-age girls.

After the war, Faith Trumbull, the older sister of Harriet and Maria, had been one of the earliest young visitors to the city. She was sent, said her father, because "she has to encounter the small Pox, as well as absence from her near Relations and Friends."[2] He apparently intended that she should be inoculated with the disease while she was in New York. Although vaccination had not yet been discovered, smallpox was known to cause far fewer deaths when induced by inoculation than when caught naturally. Yet so great was public fear that the disease might spread from patients in an inoculation hospital to the rest of the population that, until the late 1790's, many Connecticut towns refused to permit "receiving taking giving or communicating the Smallpox"[3] within their limits. By 1800, when Harriet and Maria went to New York, inoculation had become more available in their own state. But Connecticut parents had another reason to send their daughters to the city. A season in New York gave a newly "necessary" touch to a girl's education; it added a dimension to her social experience that could not be duplicated within the bounds of Connecticut.

Lebanon, where the Trumbull sisters lived, was an out-of-the-way country town about twenty miles inland from New London. For a period each spring, and whenever a thaw set in during the winter, the community was cut off from the world until the hub-deep mud dried up, froze up, or was again blanketed by snow enough for sledding. According to the Duc de Lauzun who camped his French cavalry in the middle of town during the Revolution, "Si-

2. Jonathan Trumbull, Jr. to Richard Varick, Dec. 25, 1784, New-York Historical Society, under Miscellaneous Manuscripts, Varick.

3. *The Public Records of the State of Connecticut*, Leonard W. Labaree and Catherine Fennelly, eds. (Hartford, 1951), VIII, p. 245.

beria alone can be compared to Lebanon, which is only composed of cabins scattered through immense forests."[4]

Actually Lebanon's woodlands were not so immense nor its habitations so remote and primitive as they seemed to this sophisticated Parisian. Shortly before the Revolution, Lebanon had in fact been one of Connecticut's foremost business centers. Since then, however, it had lost both population and economic status to places more conveniently located. Thus the Trumbull girls could with some justice speak of their isolation, and travelers writing about the town noted its air of decline. It did, to be sure, lie on a new turnpike route from Hartford to Norwich; but the highway, as well as being a tie to the outside world, was a constant reminder to the inhabitants that most travelers were passing Lebanon by on their way to towns of greater consequence. Nevertheless, in 1800 Lebanon still contained nearly 4000 people, most of whom supported themselves by farming. A few made leather items, cloth, and barrels which, like the agricultural produce, were hauled by oxcart and shipped through the river port of Norwich about ten miles away.

Like other New England towns, Lebanon had a central meeting house on a common surrounded by frame houses. But the common was not laid out in the customary square, triangle, or rectangle. It was a long broad ribbon over a mile in length and virtually impassable in mud time. In early spring this green barrier and the wide spacing of the houses along it frustrated sociability and added to the inhabitants' sense of isolation. Although a man could wave or shout to his neighbor next door or across the common, real talk necessitated crossing over, a trip that discouraged all but the most intrepid. Harriet and Maria were accustomed to this social barrier, since their own home, and most of those mentioned in these letters, fronted on the green. But during

4. Quoted in Rev. Robert G. Armstrong D.D., *Historic Lebanon* (Lebanon, 1950), p. 38.

most of the year the girls ran freely in and out of houses up and down the length of the string bean town, cutting across fields, zigzagging back and forth across the common, strolling by the roadside, or chasing to the point of merry collapse through the long summer grass. Life in Lebanon was simple and unpretentious. Women of means engaged in household tasks along with their servants; visiting and social gatherings were spontaneous (perhaps an impromptu dance in the kitchen, or a sleighload of young folk dropping in to thaw out); planned parties were rare. Fine houses stood next to humble ones; and social class offered no bar to neighborhood friendliness. Few people had much money, and those who did seldom showed it conspicuously.[5]

Through the years, however, Lebanon had been the home of some of Connecticut's most distinguished families. Among them, the Trumbulls had a record of eminence in public service and other fields that few families in the state could match. The father of Harriet and Maria, Jonathan Trumbull, had been governor since 1797; their grandfather (also named Jonathan) was governor from 1769 to 1784; their cousin Joseph Trumbull became governor in 1849; and their uncle John Trumbull was the well-known painter of historic scenes and great men. Yet for all their eminence, the Trumbulls fitted the easy social pattern of their town. Harriet and Maria, as these letters testify, enjoyed a warm neighborly relationship with many of the common folk. That their parents did likewise is confirmed in family letters and in a contemporary report that

plain and obscure neighbors were received [*in the Trumbull household*] with a gentle welcome, and made to feel happy in the

5. References to Lebanon throughout this volume were drawn chiefly from the following sources: letters in the Silliman Family Collection, Sterling Memorial Library at Yale University (Historical Manuscripts Collection); Rev. Orlo D. Hine, *Early Lebanon* (Hartford, 1880); D. Hamilton Hurd, *History of New London County, Connecticut* (Philadelphia, 1882); George P. Fisher, *Life of Benjamin Silliman* (Philadelphia, 1866), I, pp. 231–47.

society of those whose social position was so much superior to their own. Some persons of this description, perhaps coming from a more distant home, were received as visiting friends, and remained for several weeks at a time in the family, but they were always distinguished for personal worth.

Small farmers and mechanics not infrequently called to pass an evening hour with the girls' father, who could so well "adapt his conversation to their intelligence and circumstances that they left him with friendly and grateful feelings."[6]

In 1767, when Jonathan Trumbull was twenty-seven years old and still a budding merchant, he married Eunice Backus, daughter of Ebenezer and Eunice (Dyer) Backus. The Backus family had helped found the towns of Norwich and Windham in the seventeenth century, and ever since then Backuses had been among Connecticut's most respected and prosperous citizens.[7] They had served in town and colony government, though not on levels as high as the Trumbulls; and, like the Trumbulls, they engaged in trade. But the Backus specialty seems to have been religion, and they approached it with a zeal uncommon even in New England. Wherever a religious quarrel broke out in eighteenth-century Connecticut, a Backus was apt to be involved. Besides zealous ministers and contentious laymen, the family produced pious women. It is not surprising that one of them should have attracted Jonathan Trumbull, for the Trumbulls, too, were a religious family (Jonathan Trumbull, Senior, had almost entered the ministry and all his life had studied theology). Jonathan was not the first to be attracted

6. Quoted in Fisher, *Benjamin Silliman*, pp. 235 and 233 respectively.

7. References to the Backus family will be found in Hine, *Early Lebanon*; Hurd, *New London County*; Frances Manwaring Caulkins, *History of Norwich, Connecticut* (Hartford, 1866); Ellen D. Larned, *History of Windham County, Connecticut* (Worcester, 1880); Richard M. Bayles, *History of Windham County, Connecticut* (New York, 1889).

by a Backus; Eunice's father had won the sister of Jonathan's father, but she died young and he had twice remarried since then.

Eunice bore her husband five children, of whom only Harriet, Maria, and Faith survived infancy.[8] She was a worrier and a chronic sufferer from vague physical ailments and depressed spirits, a condition diagnosed as hypochondria and regarded in the eighteenth century as symptomatic of a malfunctioning spleen, liver, and gall bladder. Noxious vapors, it was thought, were generated in these organs and coursed upward through the body to disturb the digestion and depress the mind. Governor Trumbull and his daughters were sympathetic. Solicitude for "Mama's" worries and glooms is evident throughout the Trumbull family's correspondence and, in these letters, surely prompted Harriet and Maria to be conscientious in carrying out their instructions to write of all that befell them in New York. Their mother had never been there and was fearful that they might be contaminated by the riotous living and religious indifference of the big city.

The girls' father had been to New York often. While he served as state representative (1789–1794) and senator (1795–1796) he stopped there regularly on his way to and from the sessions of Congress at Philadelphia; and during 1789–1790, when Congress sat in New York, he lived there. Knowing the place from experience, he could not have discounted its vices nor the frivolity and dissipation of some of

8. The following vital statistics are recorded on several blank pages after the title page of the New Testament in a Bible (1803 edition) which belonged to Benjamin Silliman (Harriet's husband), Sterling Memorial Library: Jonathan Trumbull, Jr. (March 26, 1740–Aug. 7, 1809) married Eunice Backus (Aug. 1749–Feb. 3, 1826) on March 26, 1767. Their children were: Jonathan (born Dec. 24, 1767, died in infancy), Faith (Feb. 1, 1769–Oct. 19, 1840), Mary (born Dec. 27, 1777, died in infancy), Harriet (Sept. 3, 1783–Jan. 18, 1850), Maria (Feb. 14, 1785–Nov. 23, 1805).

its socially prominent citizens. Nevertheless he had many respected friends whom he could trust to provide hospitality and suitable entertainment for Harriet and Maria.

The girls were to be the paying guests of Lady Kitty Duer, who had been widowed in 1799 and reputedly was in poor financial circumstances. Governor Trumbull had know her husband, Colonel William Duer, and her father, Major-General William Alexander, during the Revolution when Trumbull was successively paymaster for the American Army, and comptroller for the American Treasury, and finally secretary to General Washington. William Duer, like Trumbull, served in several wartime roles including a stint with the Treasury. He was also one of the country's largest contractors furnishing army supplies; and it was probably in this connection that the two men became acquainted, since the Trumbull family were engaged in procuring army supplies. Jonathan's brother Joseph was commissary-general of the Continental Army until his death in 1778; and their father, as governor of Connecticut throughout the Revolution, so successfully channeled goods to the army and promoted agricultural and industrial production toward military needs that, even before the war ended, his name ("Brother Jonathan") had become legendary.[9]

After the war, Duer and Trumbull were brought together in 1789 when Trumbull was elected to Congress, and Duer was appointed assistant secretary of the Treasury. Those were the days of the "republican court" in New York, when

9. The careers of William Duer, William Alexander, and the Trumbulls are fully outlined in the *Dictionary of American Biography*. Additional useful information was found in the following: Joseph Stancliffe Davis, "William Duer, Entrepreneur, 1749–99," *Essays in the Earlier History of American Corporations* (Cambridge, 1917), I, pp. 111–338; William Alexander Duer, *William Alexander, earl of Stirling* (New York, 1847); and in Duer and Trumbull manuscripts at the Massachusetts Historical Society, the Connecticut Historical Society, the Yale University Library, the New-York Historical Society, and the Historical Society of Pennsylvania.

the first President and his lady were setting the tone of society for the new republic, holding great formal receptions at which no one dared appear who did not measure up to the proper standards of behavior and dress. Trumbull went to the Washingtons' house for dinners as well as for these large-scale gatherings; invitations came also from the Duers and from other New Yorkers whom he had met during the war. The aristocratic elegance of New York parties and the social ritual exceeded anything then to be seen in Connecticut. Permeating the manner and costume of those qualified to attend was a flavor noticeably English, perhaps because Virginia (the President's home) and New York had always had stronger connections with the mother country than the New England colonies ever developed. There was nothing in Lebanon to prepare a woman to lead such a formal social life or to dress in the appropriate high fashion, and Mrs. Trumbull's failure ever to accompany her husband to New York may have been due in part to a fear that she would not fit in.

This was a problem not simply for Mrs. Trumbull. With the emergence of the United States as a nation, Americans for the first time were brought together from every part of the country to rub elbows with one another during the sitting of Congress. They came together politically as equals but it was clear they were in other respects not equal: a farmer who had won the votes of his backwoods neighbors was not necessarily qualified to drink tea with a New York merchant or a Virginia planter. Those who came with exalted social standards did not prune them, for they were reinforced by the society of New York and Philadelphia when Congress was meeting in those cities and by the President himself. Men who came from humble communities went home with new ideas and new ambitions. The United States, they saw, though it was a republic, had not given up class distinctions, and if a legislator from a socially modest region like Connecticut wished to take a place in the national social scene equivalent to his rank at home, he and his family must learn to live gracefully in this other world.[10]

Jonathan Trumbull himself had a natural dignity and a polished yet easy manner that made him as acceptable in the highest company as he was among the humble. His social graces were combined with a character "of such acknowledged and inflexible integrity," said Elias Boudinot of New Jersey, "that he is universally beloved by all who know him."[11] Yet along with his talent for crossing social barriers, Trumbull possessed a ticklish sensitivity to his own position. There are one or two signs of it in these letters, and it was already apparent in 1778, at the time of his first entrance on the national scene, when he briefly betrayed an unbecoming concern about proper titles and forms of ad-

10. There is disagreement in contemporary diaries and letters of the 1790's (and in histories of the period) about whether or not social life in the nation's first capitals was unsuitably aristocratic for citizens of a republic. The divergent opinions reflect the different geographic and social backgrounds of the writers; but their specific descriptions of parties (clothes, menus, etc.) uniformly, and I believe reliably, indicate that some of the elite did indeed live in high style and that however simply the Washingtons lived in private, when entertaining or appearing in public they maintained standards in keeping with those of the so-called aristocratic segment of society. A variety of evidence and opinions on this subject will be found in the following: Rufus Wilmot Griswold, *The Republican Court* (New York, 1867); Frank Monaghan and Marvin Lowenthal, *This Was New York the Nation's Capital in 1789* (Garden City, N.Y. 1943); Thomas E.V. Smith, *The City of New York in the Year of Washington's Inauguration 1789* (New York, 1889); Dixon Wecter, *The Saga of American Society* (New York, 1937); Edgar S. Maclay, ed., *The Journal of William Maclay United States Senator from Pennsylvania 1789–1791* (New York, 1890); William Parker Cutler and Julia Perkins Cutler, *Life Journals and Correspondence of Rev. Manasseh Cutler LL.D.* (Cincinnati, 1888); Stewart Mitchell, ed.., *New Letters of Abigail Adams 1788–1801* (Boston, 1947); and the several works on this period by Anne Hollingsworth Wharton.

11. Milton Halsey Thomas, ed., *Elias Boudinot's Journey to Boston in 1809* (Princeton, 1955), p. 21.

dress.[12] Social sensitivity was a quirk shared by many Americans during these early days of the republic. William Maclay, a senator from Pennsylvania who bitterly resented the social slighting he received from New Yorkers, in 1789 wrote of his New England colleagues that

no people in the Union dwell more on trivial distinctions and matters of mere form. They really seem to show a readiness to stand on punctilio and ceremony. A little learning is a dangerous thing ('tis said). May not the same be said of breeding? It is certainly true that people little used with company are more apt to take offense, and are less easy, than men much versant in public life. They are an unmixed people in New England, and used only to see neighbors like themselves; and when once an error of behavior has crept in among them, there is small chance of its being cured; for, should they go abroad, being early used to a ceremonious and reserved behavior, and believing that good manners consists entirely in punctilios, they only add a few more stiffened airs to their deportment, excluding good humor, affability of conversation, and accomodation of temper and sentiment as qualities too vulgar for a gentleman.[13]

If the New Englanders in New York and Philadelphia seemed to overvalue manners and punctilios, it was perhaps not simply a case of provincialism but because they were trying to accommodate to a social environment that appeared to them to dwell upon niceties. Harriet and Maria Trumbull were obviously doing their Connecticut best to accommodate, as they made their calls and drank their tea in the New York of 1801. But there were limits. New Englanders were proud of their ways (which they described in terms quite different from Maclay's), and they were intent on preserving them. Nevertheless, New Englanders also meant to have their due and recognized that to get it they

12. See Henry Laurens, Jr. to Jonathan Trumbull, Jr., Feb. [March] 12, 1778; Oliver Wolcott to Mrs. Wolcott, April 14, 1778; and Oliver Wolcott to Jonathan Trumbull Jr., May 18, 1778 in Edmund C. Burnett, ed., *Letters of Members of the Continental Congress*, (8 vols., Washington, 1921–1936), III, pp. 126, 167, 253.

13. *Journal of William Maclay*, p. 5. *See also* pp. 305 and 352.

might have to learn a thing or two that could be learned only outside New England. Jonathan Trumbull had had the opportunity during the Revolution when General Washington, Lord Stirling, and the aristocratic Duer and Hamilton had been his associates; and in 1790–1791, when he attended Congress in Philadelphia, his daughter Faith had been there with him absorbing the ways and outlook of this larger society.[14]

Governor Trumbull could do no less for his other daughters in 1800. Harriet, at seventeen, was suffering from an over-concern for propriety and a diffidence unsuited to her station. Fifteen-year-old Maria, though endowed with a blithe disposition that would carry her through any situation, nevertheless needed training that her mother could not give. Because they were Trumbulls and could expect to play a role either in the larger world outside Connecticut or in the new society that upper-class Connecticut was developing in conformity to that world, Governor Trumbull apparently believed that his daughters needed the social schooling that New York had to offer.

Lady Catherine Alexander Duer—better known as Lady Kitty—was well qualified to provide it. She was related to some of New York's oldest patrician families and even claimed nobility in her own right, but the House of Lords, many years earlier, had denied her father's right of succession to the vacant Scottish earldom of Stirling. William Alexander was, after all, an American; and James Alexander, his father, who fled to America in 1716, had been a rebel—a partisan of the deposed Stuart kings. Nevertheless, after making his unsuccessful bid for the title, William Alexander for the rest of his life was known as Lord Stirling, and his wife and daughters were addressed as "Lady." The con-

14. Jeremiah Wadsworth and Oliver Ellsworth (both from Connecticut) also had daughters there. Isaac Bronson (also spelled Brunson) to Mrs. Bronson, Philadelphia, Jan. 1, 1791, Murray Papers Box 3, New-York Historical Society.

tinuance of this deference after the Revolution may seem unbecoming for a people who had just repudiated monarchy, created a republic, and forbidden themselves to accept titles from foreign governments. But it was a just reflection of the existing upper-class pride in social distinctions and, by a characteristically American mode of reasoning, it was also an indignant repudiation of Parliament's inference that Americans were not worthy of British titles.

Had Lady Kitty Alexander not been already on the top rung of the social ladder, her marriage (in 1779—General Washington gave the bride away) to William Duer would have placed her there. He was an engaging English-born gentleman of substantial fortune who came to America on business in 1768 and decided to stay. Like all such recent immigrants he was a welcome addition to society, for upper-class New York depended on them to keep it abreast of English manners and mores. Some people thought William Duer a financial wizard; but others recognized (as modern scholars do) an overambitious promoter and speculator who manipulated government bonds and lands for private profit, and who juggled funds that existed only on paper. In 1792 these talents finally brought about his downfall and precipitated the first major business panic in the United States, a catastrophe so extensive, according to one contemporary account, "as to affect not only private Credit from Georgia to New Hampshire inclusive; but even the public Debt & Credit of the United States."[15]

New York was hardest hit. Men and women on every level of society suffered, and frantic letters poured out of the city.

15. Richard Platt to Winthrop Sargent, March 25, 1792, Sargent Papers, Massachusetts Historical Society. Although Duer was widely blamed for causing the panic of 1792, his own business failure was but a precipitating agency. Many other men had shared equally in creating a dangerous financial situation.

> We have the devil to pay! *Col. Duer* has failed for they say three millions of dollars, and has taken in almost every person in the city, from the richest merchants to even the poorest women, and the little shopkeepers, women, and butchers. He is now in the new jail and they even talk of breaking it open to take him out and tear him piecemeal, and to hang every indorser of his notes if everything is not shortly settled. How it will end God only knows.[16]

There was rioting, and business came to a halt for lack of both money and credit. While the financial confusion lasted, and for seven years thereafter, William Duer remained in the debtors' prison. On May 7, 1799 he died there, just as his years of negotiation to obtain a release seemed about to succeed.

In 1801 when the Trumbull girls came to New York, the name of William Duer could still arouse rancor in certain quarters and was being used specifically for that purpose in some city newspapers.[17] Despite her husband's role in the financial calamity and her resultant straitened circumstances, the fact remained that Lady Kitty was related by blood or marriage to almost every family of social consequence in the city.[18] Furthermore, since the financial practices of a number of wealthy New Yorkers were identical with William Duer's, they were less inclined to censure him

16. From a letter dated March 29, 1792, in Thomas Jones, *History of New York During the Revolutionary War*, ed. Edward Floyd De Lancey (New York, 1879), II, p. 589.

17. *The Republican Watch-Tower* on April 25, 1801 carried a letter (signed Nestor) denouncing Hamilton's financial program as "a millstone about the neck of poor America. . . . every Clerk in the Treasury of the United States knows it [*the funding system*] was the child of Col. Duer, who was the Foreman to cut out the pattern for the Journeymen to stick together, and finally for Mr. Hamilton to finish by running his goose (quill) over the seams, in his Maiden Report of 1789. . . ." See also *The American Citizen*, April 18, 1801, article signed "Nassau."

18. Lady Kitty (whose mother was Sarah Livingston, daughter of Catherine Van Brugh and Philip, second Lord of Livingston Manor)

than to pity his bad luck. Lady Kitty could no longer afford to live on Broadway or in any other genteel neighborhood. She kept no carriage, employed no galaxy of servants, and did not entertain in the old Duer manner, but she continued to lead a busy social life.

From Governor Trumbull's viewpoint, the Duer household must have seemed an especially suitable environment for his daughters, because it was full of young people close to their age. Lady Kitty had eight children: the oldest, John and William (eighteen and twenty respectively) were preparing for legal careers; the others, in order of birth, were Frances, Sarah, Catherine, Maria, Henrietta, and Alexander, who was born in 1793 after his father's imprisonment. As guests in the Duer family the Trumbull girls would presumably be introduced to Lady Kitty's friends and to her children's numerous young cousins and their friends and elders. Through such contacts "social schooling" was accomplished. The grooming, fashion, and etiquette proper for various occasions had to be learned from experience, from observation and emulation, and from guidance by someone who knew.

If Harriet and Maria came to New York expecting such guidance from Lady Kitty, they soon realized their mistake. She did offer some advice, and the girls did meet her friends and relatives, but Lady Kitty was too busy mending her own life to lead them by the hand. She was in fact being courted by a wealthy merchant, William Neilson (also spelled Nelson), who married her not long after Harriet and Maria returned to Connecticut.

---

had four paternal and eight maternal aunts and uncles whose marriages provided her with dozens of cousins. The marriages of her cousins produced a staggering ramification of family connections. See Elizabeth Clarkson Jay, "The Descendants of James Alexander," *New York Genealogical and Biographical Record,* XII (1881), pp. 13–28; and Edwin Brockholst Livingston *The Livingstons of Livingston Manor* (New York, 1910), appendices G, H, I.

Maria thrived in her new environment, but Harriet during these months suffered an anguish barely hinted at in the letters she wrote to her parents. Several years later she revealed it to a friend who complained of shyness:

> You should endeavour by occasionally visiting with your Mama, to overcome some of that reluctance you have to going in company, beleive me you will find less difficulty in doing it now, than in a year or two hence, and you will save yourself many disagreeable embarressments. I have experienced as many awkward feelings as any one, arising from a foolish diffidence, which I think might in great measure have been prevented, if I had lived in a situation where I might have been introduced into company by my Mother or Sister when young, instead of going from the retired life we lead at Lebanon, to New York with a younger Sister where we were left to take care of ourselves.[19]

Harriet's hint of neglect is not wholly warranted by the contents of the letters she and Maria wrote from New York. Although Lady Kitty and her circle were sometimes less attentive than the girls thought appropriate, the rest of their father's friends were very helpful and actually offered more hospitality than the girls accepted. Perhaps because of the formality of some of their initial social encounters, they assumed that it would not be proper to pursue a proffered friendship unless it was accompanied by an invitation for a specific time. This was a safe general maxim, but one that the best people often broke; for all the formal calling and party-going that went on in the city, New Yorkers themselves also unceremoniously dropped in on each other ("in a friendly way" as they put it) or on the spur of the moment brought friends home for dinner or tea if they chanced to meet.[20] But how could Harriet and Maria have known that?

19. Harriet Trumbull to Eliza Sebor, April 23, 1804, Silliman Family Collection. Harriet here exaggerates her inexperience. Her Connecticut visiting had included Hartford, the home of her married sister.

20. See the diary of Elizabeth DeHart Bleeker, 1799–1806 *passim*. Manuscript in New York Public Library.

Their modest New England country upbringing made them feel uncomfortably out of place in grand surroundings, fearful of committing social blunders, and perhaps oversensitive in detecting social slights. Without the protective company of someone who knew the ways of the city, they were understandably reluctant to call often on the great ladies who led lives conspicuously different from their own.

### *The Economic Scene*

Though Harriet and Maria at times moved among the aristocrats of New York, their main experience was with people not very different from those they knew at home—people who had in fact come from Connecticut, but not as visitors. Of the approximately thirty-eight New York families or individuals with whom the girls established social relations, twenty-five had emigrated from Connecticut. Ever since the 1760's and 1770's when the colony's tillable acreage began to seem inadequate to its growing population, people had been heading out in many directions. Most of those who left were farmers aiming for unoccupied land in the Vermont area, upper New York, and beyond. But after the Revolution merchants also felt compelling reasons to depart, and their destination was usually New York.

The Connecticut merchants began moving into New York shortly after the British evacuation in 1783, when the future of commerce in their own state suddenly turned black, and the exodus continued as the difficulties of trade multiplied. The chief market for Connecticut's agricultural products had always been the British and French colonies in the West Indies, and with the return of peace everyone had expected also the return of trade to this prosperous prewar channel. Instead, when American independence was established, England instituted restrictions against American trade with British colonies; and France and Spain revoked privileges formerly allowed to Americans dealing with their possessions. In spite of these handicaps, trade with the West Indies, even illicit trade, was resumed as far as possible, for Connecticut's economy had somehow to be sustained while new avenues of commerce were being sought out.

As well as losing markets the merchants had lost ships. Norwich alone, in the ten-year period preceding 1801, reported the seizure of over a hundred merchantmen owned in that port.[21] Pirates operating in the Mediterranean accounted for some of these, but the heaviest spoliations took place in the West Indies. American ships trading there had been seized from time to time for entering forbidden ports; but the number of seizures soared after 1793 when England and France went to war and each tried to prevent American supplies from going to the other. The United States government took counter-measures so far as it was able, and for a time was virtually at war with France. By 1801 relations with the belligerents had ironed out considerably. Yet even while Harriet and Maria were in New York, the newspapers reported that the United States frigate *Philadelphia*, during three days off Guadeloupe, had retaken four seized American schooners, three of which were from New London, Connecticut.[22]

All the while that merchants in Connecticut were coping with the difficulties of the West Indies trade, they were watching merchants in New York grow wealthy by the importation and distribution of British manufactures. A handsome profit was to be reaped from selling English goods in states like Connecticut whose vessels, for the most part, did not trade in England. It made sense, then, if the opportunity arose, for an ambitious merchant to abandon Connecticut and its dependence on the West Indies for the

21. *Republican Watch-Tower*, April 28, 1801.
22. *Ibid.*, Feb. 18, 1801.

broader and more lucrative field of operations available in New York.[23]

When the migration began, if a Connecticut man was well supplied with capital and had dealt with New York firms enough to become familiar with their business practices, he could make the move independently; otherwise he entered into partnership with a native New York merchant. If after a few years the partners split into two firms (as was characteristic of American business partnerships during this period), the Connecticut man often invited a Connecticut friend or relative to come to New York and join him in a new partnership. In time this firm might also split and become the nucleus for two more new partnerships to be filled by men from back home. The pattern was repeated often enough to make New York's community of ex-Connecticut merchants widely interrelated. But it was by no means inbred: the children had been growing up and marrying into New York families; and sometimes the children's Connecticut cousins and friends found New York husbands and wives when they came to visit.[24]

Such interstate marriages were increasing not only in New York and Connecticut, but throughout the United States, for many aspects of life in the new nation brought

23. For a general discussion of the commerce of New York see Sidney I. Pomerantz, *New York: an American City 1783–1803* (New York, 1938), pp. 147–60. A detailed description of spoliations and other trade difficulties besetting Connecticut is in Caulkins, *History of Norwich*, pp. 473–502.

24. This paragraph and succeeding ones about ex-Connecticut merchants are based on material drawn from the following sources: manuscripts of merchants mentioned in these letters; advertisements in New York and Connecticut newspapers; birth and marriage records of New York and Connecticut (Barbour Index at State Library in Hartford); standard genealogical works; and histories of Connecticut towns and New York cited in other footnotes of this volume. J. A. Scoville (Walter Barrett, clerk, pseud.), *The Old Merchants of New York City* (5 vols. New York, 1863–1870) provides valuable leads but its accuracy is unreliable.

men and women from different parts of the country together. The senators, representatives, and other officers who assembled to run the national government sometimes brought along their wives or their older children. Stagecoach and packet service and roads had improved immeasurably, making it easier for young ladies like Harriet and Maria to spend a season in New York or Philadelphia or Boston, and for merchants themselves to travel on business instead of relying on letters or on supercargoes and the captains of trading vessels. Moreover, business itself was expanding and broadening the association of Americans with one another.

As individual enterprises grew larger in scale and as corporations, in organizing themselves, reached out for members with capital to invest, business increasingly spanned state lines. The merchants who moved from Connecticut to New York, for instance, seldom completely severed their old economic ties. The owner of a going concern, instead of dissolving it when he left, might have a partner run it. One of the advantages of moving to New York was, after all, the profit to be made from selling British goods to an already established network of business connections in Connecticut. The expatriate merchants from Connecticut also had potentially valuable connections in the new western settlements beyond the boundaries of the existing states. These were more readily accessible from New York (via the Hudson River) than from Connecticut, and many of them were being founded by pioneers from Connecticut who welcomed dealing with men from their home state.

Of course not everyone made the grade in New York business. Some failed, or barely managed to hang on, or gave up and went home, or moved west. But on the whole, the ex-Connecticut merchants who appear in these letters were a remarkably successful lot. Those who had arrived first, like Moses Rogers and James Watson, already stood in the first rank of New York businessmen; and the younger men who had come later were fast catching up, for as business expansion accelerated fortunes were made sooner. Merchants from other parts of New England emigrated to New York with similar success, luring more to follow them until in the middle of the nineteenth century New York commerce was virtually dominated by former Yankees.[25] Among them, the men who had arrived from Connecticut in the eighteenth century (and their sons and grandsons) continued to hold a prominent place.

Since the expansion of social and economic relations between New York and Connecticut during the last seventeen years of the eighteenth century is one of the significant but unspoken developments that can be gleaned from the names scattered through the Trumbull girls' letters, the footnotes will call attention to all people from Connecticut, whether they were permanent residents or visitors to the city. In New York at the same time as Harriet and Maria there were Connecticut merchants who had come on temporary business, young Connecticut men who were being initiated into the commercial world by working in city firms, and Connecticut girls who were visiting friends and relatives who had moved out of their home state. The presence of this enclave of ex-Connecticut families was undoubtedly a factor in Governor Trumbull's decision to send his daughters to the city, since the men were almost all business or personal friends of his who would feel some obligation toward his children.

### *The Political Scene*

When the Trumbull girls arrived in New York in December 1800, the city, the state, and the nation were on the verge of a political revolution which many people feared

25. The nineteenth century infiltration by New Englanders is described in Robert Greenhalgh Albion, "Yankee Domination of New York Port 1820–1865," *New England Quarterly*, V (1932), pp. 665–98;

might override electoral channels and result in civil war: the Federalists, who had controlled the national government since its institution in 1789, were about to be swept out of office by the Republicans. In February the Republicans defeated President John Adams at the polls and placed Thomas Jefferson in his chair; in April, after capturing the governorship of New York with its numerous appointive offices, they began to oust the local Federalist bureaucracy. Inasmuch as the merchants of the city were, with few exceptions, Federalists and frequently officeholders, the political axe fell more than once on the Trumbulls' friends. Governor Trumbull was of course a Federalist, too.

Both parties waged virulent election campaigns with a mounting hysteria among the Federalists as the Republicans slashed ahead to success. Every Federalist newspaper in the country published editorials, articles, and letters about the villainous Republicans, the threat they posed to morals, religion, and good government, and the imminence of violence. On September 29, 1800, for example, a lurid piece in the *Connecticut Courant* warned readers to

> Look at your houses, your parents, your wives, and your children. Are you prepared to see your dwellings in flames, hoary hairs bathed in blood, female chastity violated, or children writhing on the pike and halberd? If not, prepare for the task of protecting your Government. Look at every leading Jacobin [*used as a smear word for Republicans*] as at a ravening wolf, preparing to enter your peaceful fold, and glut his deadly appetite on the vitals of your Country.

In the same issue a more moderate article claimed that:

> Jacobins hate our holy religion, because it humbles the pride of human reason, and prescribes purity of life, and manners. . . . Let it be remembered that the Jacobin creed . . . denies the being of a God—the necessity of virtue, either for public or private

---

see also W.R. Hopkins, "Beginnings of the New England Society of New York," *Magazine of American History*, XI (1884), pp. 33–37.

happiness,—it discards the inviolability of the marriage tie. . . . Is it strange that under the impressions of such a creed, man should become a ferocious savage, warring on all which in civilized society has been revered as pure, lovely, and of good report.

That debauchery was characteristic of Republicans was the keynote sounded by Federalists newspapers everywhere, and after the elections they pointed to bibulous Republican victory celebrations as fulfillment of their claims. To this charge, New York's *Republican Watch-Tower* retorted "That there are some debauched characters who stile themselves republicans, cannot be denied; but that intoxication is the *peculiar* habit of democracy, can and will be denied.—Have we never seen aristocrats deviate from the paths of sobriety? Have we never seen riots and drunken mobs, on Federal jubilees?"[26]

Connecticut Federalists, like other earnest politicians before and since, were half-persuaded by their own propaganda. To the governor in Connecticut the situation in New York looked far more menacing than it did to his friends and daughters who were actually in the city, and at one point he even concluded that it would no longer be safe for Harriet and Maria to remain there. A letter from Philadelphia received by a family friend seemed to confirm the governor's fears of impending civil war. Elihu Chauncy had attended, incognito, a "Democratic meeting" where "they talked openly of settling the differences of party by the point of the bayonet, and their conduct and conversation evidently showed that they stood ready to cut our throats at the first signal."[27]

If Republicans fell to cutting throats, the governor

26. *Republican Watch-Tower*, March 7, 1801, incorrectly dated Wednesday, March 4.

27. Elihu Chauncey to Benjamin Silliman, Philadelphia, Jan. 30, 1801, quoted in Fisher, *Benjamin Silliman*, p. 68. Silliman was a close friend of Daniel Wadsworth, the governor's son-in-law. See also James Hillhouse to Jonathan Trumbull, Philadelphia, Feb. 3, 1801, Trumbull Correspondence I, Connecticut Historical Society.

wanted his daughters safe in Lebanon. But even in Connecticut, he worried about the April elections. Hitherto Connecticut had been a Federalist stronghold, and the Trumbull girls did not seriously consider the possibility that their father might be ousted from the governor's chair during their absence. Governor Trumbull himself could not afford to be so complacent. Though Connecticut was justifiably reputed throughout the nation as the land of steady political habits, the Republicans were fortified in this election by the fact that the Federalists had been pursuing national policies that antagonized a large part of the American population. No local Federalist politician, however popular, could tell how strongly this antagonism against the Federalist national government might redound against himself. Moreover, the Connecticut Republicans in this election campaign had been receiving outside help with propaganda and organizational tactics. Aaron Burr, the Republican vice-presidential candidate, came from New York on an advisory tour, and New York's Republican press launched a scurrilous attack to persuade Connecticut voters to break the Federalists' grip on their state legislature.

Although they were naturally indignant at this outside interference, the Connecticut Federalists had themselves been writing anti-Republican propaganda for circulation in other states.[28] Furthermore one of the most ardent anti-Re-

28. The Connecticut writers particularly resented by the Republicans were the Rev. Timothy Dwight, his brother Theodore, Noah Webster, Jr., David Daggett, Dr. Lemuel Hopkins, John Trumbull (the poet-lawyer; not the uncle of Harriet and Maria Trumbull), the Rev. Jedidiah Morse, and Warren Dutton. The latter two were at the time living in Massachusetts where Dutton, a former Yale tutor, had just become editor of a new and extreme Federalist newspaper, *The Mercury and New England Palladium*, which (said the Republicans) had been fathered by Dwight and Morse and was the mouthpiece through which they broadcast to the rest of the country. See letters and editorials Jan.–May 1801 *passim* in *American Citizen*, *Republican Watch-Tower*, and *American Mercury* (Hartford), especially April 23.

publicans in the whole country, and a most influential one, was the Reverend Timothy Dwight, president of Yale College. Dwight was certain that Republicans were anti-Christian (because of their sympathy for the French Revolution), and the rest of the Connecticut clergy, almost to a man, reflected his views and believed it their duty to warn the public against irreligious (i.e. Republican) candidates for office. Dwight went to New York at the end of January to preach[29] and, as the New York Republicans believed, to forward the Federalist cause. They retaliated by denouncing ministers who played politics, and they urged the people of Connecticut to cease being the dupes of Federalist priests and politicians. According to one article, the boasted "steady political habits" of the state arose simply from the tyrannical practice of deifying a man as soon as he was elected to public office and condemning "as blasphemous every person who should presume to question his integrity, or examine his conduct."[30]

Republicans were convinced that the Federalism of Dwight and his fellow clergymen was motivated by personal ambition; and they could not refrain from a bit of crowing when the Federalists lost the presidential election. On May 16, 1801, the *Republican Watch-Tower* in New York carried the following snide letter:

To his Holiness Pope Timothy the first, President of a certain College not more than a thousand miles from the City of New-Haven in Connecticut.

HOLY FATHER

The illusion is at length dispelled, thy wayward fancy which has for years been dreaming of the establishment of a national religion, wherein thou

29. The diary of Elizabeth Bleeker records hearing Dwight preach on Jan. 25, 1801; and the *Republican Watch-Tower* on Jan. 28 announced that "On Wednesday last arrived in town his Holiness the *Pope of Connecticut.*"

30. *Republican Watch-Tower*, March 25, 1801.

wast to play the part of chief hierarch; thy associating and consociating imagination, which had figured to thee a Mitre suspended over thy meek and holy head, . . . thy splendid vision of a national university, over which thou wast to preside, . . . all, all are quash'd, quash'd Timothy, quash'd. . . . Thou can'st no longer aspire to promotion by theologic politics . . . for promotion Timothy no longer cometh from the East. Braintree [*the home of ex-president John Adams*] and Yale, will no longer chuckle together . . . John Adams will not have it in his power to reward thee with an archi-congregational palace—Thy attentions will be confined to the superintendance of thy puritanical college, where thy Hopkinsian lectures on divinity may find a devoted admirer in some N. England, praise God bare bones.

Actually Timothy Dwight's efforts did not go unrewarded. His own state remained firmly Federalist, and Governor Trumbull was reelected every year until his death in 1809.

### *The Religious Scene*

The Republicans were unquestionably right in claiming that the religious aspects of the election were important in Connecticut, and their anti-clerical propaganda may even have helped the Connecticut Federalists by exemplifying the irreverence which the ministers had conditioned the public to expect from Republicans. In spite of a general decline in piety throughout the country, the people of Connecticut were still a remarkably religious lot. The Trumbull girls plainly carried with them to New York the New Englander's persistent appetite for preaching. That their mother was a pious woman stands out in many letters, and the piety of Governor Trumbull was considered noteworthy by his contemporaries. Since the Trumbulls, like the vast majority of Connecticut people, were Congregationalists, a word of explanation is needed about why Harriet and Maria attended the Anglican church while they were in New York.

The answer lies in the fact that by 1801 piety in Connecticut was not necessarily accompanied by bigotry. The

Trumbulls, like a number of Connecticut Congregationalists, had liberal views of other denominations. These views came to them through Jonathan Trumbull's father and through the Reverend Zebulon Ely, minister of their church. Both had been good friends and admirers of the Reverend Ezra Stiles who, as president of Yale before Timothy Dwight, had a religious (and political) perspective far too broad to please most Connecticut clergymen. The elder Governor Trumbull had usually stayed with Stiles when the legislature met in New Haven; and Ely, who had attended college under Stiles, so admired the irenical president that he named his first-born son Ezra Stiles. The Trumbulls' tolerance was also nourished by living in a town that contained a number of non-Congregational families; not every community did. Furthermore, nearby Norwich and New London each had enough Anglican families to support an Anglican church and among the members were merchant friends and kin of the Trumbulls. It would seem that there was an affinity between Anglicanism and commerce, for the denomination was concentrated in commercial towns though thin-spread through most of Connecticut. More than likely, Harriet and Maria Trumbull sometimes accompanied friends to the Anglican church when visiting in Norwich. Liberal Congregationalists felt no qualms about doing so under special circumstances; and certainly nothing in the girls' letters suggests that their attendance at the Anglican church while living in New York was a novel experience.

It is, nevertheless, a little surprising that they should have attended that church regularly. There were, to be sure, no Congregational churches in New York. But there were several Presbyterian congregations whose theology was identical with the Congregationalists', and there were churches of other denominations that were equally Calvinist in doctrine. Moreover, the girls had friends who attended Presbyterian services and might have taken them along. But for a Yankee, the Calvinist churches of New York did have one serious drawback. They generally got their clergy from New Jersey or Pennsylvania where the style in preaching was quite different from New England's. Abigail Adams, the President's wife, described hearing New York ministers whose oratory "consists in foaming, loud speaking, working themselves up in such an enthusiasm as to cry" or "who preach without Notes . . . and whose Noise and vehemince is to compensate for every other difficency." She longed for "devotion without grimace." After a series of unsatisfactory Sundays she wrote to her sister back in Massachusetts:

I have sometimes gone to St. Pauls [*Anglican church*]. There I find much more liberal discourses, but bred a desenter and approveing that mode of worship, I feel reluctance at changing tho I would always go to church [*i.e., an Anglican church*], if I resided where there was no other mode of worship. The [*Calvinist*] Clergymen here I am told are so Rigid that their company is very little sought after. They never mix with their people as they do with us, and there is in there Air and countanances that solemn Phiz and gate which looks so like mummery that instead of Reverence they create disgust, and they address their Audience with so much self importance and Priestly despotism that I am really surprizd at their having any men of sense and abilities for their hearers. I have seen but one exception to this character and that in a Dr. Lynd who is really the best and most liberal of the whole sett.[31]

Perhaps Governor Trumbull shared Mrs. Adams' opinion of the Calvinist clergy in New York and advised his daughters to worship with the Anglicans. Or he may have suggested it simply as a broadening experience or because Har-

31. Letters dated Oct. 4, 1789 and July 4, 1790 in *New Letters of Abigail Adams*, pp. 27, 53. Mrs. Adams and Jonathan Trumbull had little oportunity to hear the universally esteemed Dr. John Rodgers who was in ill health during the winter that they were in New York for the meeting of Congress, and by the time Harriet and Maria visited the city the old minister seldom preached any more.

riet and Maria were to be living in an Anglican family.[32] Whatever the reason, the question must have been settled before the girls left home for they apparently felt no need for explanation in their letters.

*The New York Scene*

Life in New York was a far cry from life in quiet Lebanon —streets full of people, paved streets with sidewalks; houses close packed, even wall to wall; dozens of shops to visit, lessons to attend, social obligations to fulfill; and for diversion, a ball, a party, a play, or a concert. The excitement of it all and the busyness even submerged Harriet's homesickness for a while. The girls traveled several miles on foot each day making their social rounds, which may be followed on the accompanying map (addresses of the people they visited are included in the footnotes). But anyone familiar with present-day New York will scarcely be able to visualize the scene in 1801; New York, with a population of 60,000, occupied only the tip of Manhattan Island. Houses extended for not much more than a mile from the Battery along the Hudson River and for approximately twice that distance along the East River. Between was a web of cross streets; beyond was open country, studded here and there with the summer homes of wealthy citizens. Up the east side of the island, but inland, ran the highway to Boston; and beside the Hudson a lesser road led out to the village of Greenwich. But the great Broadway, which started out wide and handsome from the Battery, soon narrowed

32. Without specific substantiating evidence it would be rash to jump to the conclusion that social class or politics influenced the Trumbulls' choice of church. Although many New York Republicans were both working class and Calvinist and although New York's inauguration day ceremony was held in a Calvinist church, it was also true that many New York Federalists were Calvinists and that a sizable part of New York's upper crust was Calvinist—including people mentioned in these letters.

down to little more than a farmers' lane cutting across private property, up and down caterpillar hills, through low wet meadowland, and finally intersected a sandy cross-island track that ran between the Boston road and Greenwich and on up the west side of the island.[33]

Lady Kitty's house was in the west side on Chambers Street, which crossed Broadway about where the city began to give way to meadow. Though respectable, the street was far from fashionable. The almshouse was there, and it backed on the city jail. The neighborhood was also inconveniently remote from the shopping district and from the homes of the Trumbull girls' friends. New York's more prosperous citizens preferred to live close to the business center and some, as had been the custom in the past, still kept house in the building where they did business.

When emerging from Chambers Street, Harriet and Maria turned down rather than up Broadway. Everyone and everything they wanted to see lay in that direction. Besides, countryward the street was ungraded and muddy, while cityward it was wonderfully broad, paved, and flanked by brick sidewalks all the way. For much of its length the shops and houses were still new enough to show their newness, and more were under construction. During the British army's occupation of New York a disastrous fire (1776) destroyed nearly a thousand buildings, mostly along Broadway and west to the Hudson River. The area had lain

33. The references most helpful for discovering the character of New York in 1801 were I.N. Phelps Stokes, *The Iconography of Manhattan Island* (6 vols., New York, 1915–1928); *Minutes of the Common Council of the City of New York 1784–1801* (New York, 1917), I and II; Martha J. Lamb, *History of the City of New York* (New York and Chicago, 1880), II; James Grant Wilson, ed. *The Memorial History of the City of New York* (New York, 1893), III and IV; Rodman Gilder, *The Battery* (Boston, 1936); Samuel Wood, *The Cries of New York* (New York, 1931); Pomerantz, *New York an American City*; and the contemporary newspapers and manuscripts cited throughout the present volume.

in ruin throughout the war, and afterward reconstruction had been delayed by depression. But within the twelve years preceding 1800 building had so boomed that even houses which survived the conflagration were demolished to make room for more imposing new ones. Wealthy merchants had begun to want elegant residences apart from their businesses, and Broadway had become a highly-favored address. A few years after the Trumbull girls' visit an English traveler compared Broadway to Oxford Street, describing the lofty, English-style houses which, he said, differed little from those of London's West End "except that they are universally built of red brick."[34]

Since Broadway ran along the height of land roughly parallel to the two rivers and sloped gently but steadily uphill all the way to Chambers Street, the girls caught a glimpse of sails and water at almost every cross street as they walked down to the Battery, their most frequent destination. The first block on their route was a long one, bordered by a wooden fence enclosing the city prison. Next came the triangular Park or Common. The prison faced the Common, and in the street that ran between them a horse auction took place on some days. Looking across the green from Broadway toward the third side of the triangle, one could see the Park Theater and the Brick Presbyterian Church (the locale of Republican festivities on the day of President Jefferson's inauguration), and soon after passing the end of the Common one came to St. Paul's Chapel. St. Paul's was one of the few buildings in the burnt-out area that the firefighters had been able to save. Trinity Church, six blocks farther on, had been consumed; but a new Trinity, on the same site, had been consecrated in 1790, and Harriet and Maria regularly attended here each Sunday afternoon. In the morning they went to St. Paul's.

34. Quoted in Lamb, *History of the City of New York*, II, p. 435.

Walking down Broadway on weekdays, the closer one approached to the commercial districts the busier and noisier the scene became. New York had a huge population of cartmen engaged in moving goods to and from the wharves, and they depended as much on their raucous voices as on their reins when guiding their horses through congested areas. The sound of wheels and of voices was one of the inescapable facts of life in New York, "this great hencoop of a city," as Maria called it. Besides the bellowing cartmen there were vendors with handcarts, goat carts, and dog carts who trudged up one street and down the next advertising their wares as far away as their voices would carry. Their singsong calls, formalized and repetitive, melodious and cacophonous, echoed in various keys from different sectors of the city, counterpointed by the clatter of horses' hoofs, the rattle of light chaise wheels, and the rumble of heavy oxcarts. The noise of New York was remarkable even to New Yorkers, and everyone welcomed the comparative hush that fell over the city when a heavy snow brought out sleighs to replace wheeled vehicles.

Sometimes Harriet and Maria turned off Broadway to shop in the side streets or on William Street, the favorite fashion-hunting ground of New York ladies. Bowed-front glass windows for exhibiting merchandise were the latest architectural innovation that winter, and they were much hailed because they "will make the street of business appear very handsome, and preclude the necessity of exposing goods for sale over the walks."[35] Buildings in this vicinity were generally brick or brickfronted, and roofed with tile, materials which provided some protection against flying brands spewed forth by great fires (like the one mentioned by Maria) that now and again struck fear and dreadful memories in every New York heart. It was possible to go

35. *The Spectator,* May 30, 1801.

directly from the shopping district to the Battery, but the neighborhood was none too good and the girls probably preferred to walk straight down Broadway. A few blocks past Trinity Church the houses diverged to form a broad open triangle with a fenced bowling green in the center. Overlooking the green, from a fifteen-foot hillock at the far end, stood the customhouse, an impressive pillared and porticoed building that had been constructed to house the president of the United States when New York expected to be the nation's capital. Beyond lay the Battery, sloping to the water and wrapping around the southern tip of Manhattan island.

The Battery occupied the grounds of the old British Fort George which had been razed in 1790. The city had since graded the land, laid out paths and terraces, set out trees, and constructed a sea wall along which—a grim reminder of still troubled times—stretched a bastion of stone, planks, and posts that New York citizens of every social class had helped to build in 1798, when attack by France seemed certain. Although the bastion somewhat marred the looks of the broad walk that ran along the waterfront, the Battery was still the city's favorite promenade, and out-of-town visitors went there to watch the ships entering and leaving the great harbor and to admire the ladies who habitually strolled there in the early evening. Despite the popularity of the Battery, a continuous effort was necessary to maintain it as a proper park; as late as 1808 the city government was petitioned to keep out cows and other animals, and to prevent the beating of carpets and the spreading of clothes within the grounds. New York was still young when Harriet and Maria Trumbull walked her streets.

### *The Cultural Scene*

Sightseeing was of course not the Trumbull girls' primary object in going to New York. They were to learn what genteel New York girls learned, and that meant—in addition to gaining social experience—acquiring appropriate clothes, and skill in dancing, drawing, and music.

Dancing, drawing, and music were slow to find a place in the cultural life of Connecticut, partly because teachers and money were scarce but also because people harbored an ancestral prejudice against time spent in useless activities. Nevertheless, during the preceding dozen or so years a surge of interest in the arts had engulfed the state and created a steady rise in the ranks of those who could make music and of those who wanted to learn. Enthusiasm, hard practice, and the missionary zeal of proficient amateurs made up for what was lacking in professional instruction, and resulted in the formation of choirs, bands, and chamber groups. Upper-class parents began to think of music and drawing as desirable equipment for their daughters, and some schools for girls began to offer lessons.[36] Harriet and Maria were lucky in having an artist for an uncle. Furthermore, in 1797 while visiting their married sister Faith Wadsworth in Hartford, they were able to take drawing lessons from a Miss Wells, an English lady who kept a school there. In 1801, however, art and music instruction remained in the hands of amateurs except in the largest towns, where a transient master might settle down to teach for a few months at a time.

Although dancing schools had for years been actively opposed in Connecticut, and only twelve years earlier a dancing master who tried to give classes in New Haven had been run out of town,[37] by 1801 lessons had become available in many places; and, as in the case of music, they were conducted by traveling teachers. Since Harriet and Maria were evidently not beginners, they had probably been permitted

36. See, for example, the advertisement for Mrs. Brooks's "Ladies' Boarding and Day School" in Norwich, *Connecticut Courant,* Jan. 6, 1800; and Laura Hadley Moseley, ed., *The Diaries of Julia Cowles* (New Haven, 1931), pp. 27. 28, 30.

37. Edmund S. Morgan, *The Gentle Puritan: A Life of Ezra Stiles 1727–1795* (New Haven, 1962), p. 421.

to attend the classes of John C. Devero, who in 1797 began teaching in Norwich and other towns near Lebanon. Most Dancing schools in the United States at this time were run by Frenchmen, who advertised that they taught not merely dancing but "polite manners," which meant deportment in the ballroom and such things as how gracefully to sit, rise, walk, bow, curtsy, and even how properly to flourish a handkerchief. Emphasis on the teaching of manners was one way to combat popular prejudice in places like Connecticut, where John Devero, for example, advertised that inasmuch as he "pays the greatest attention to the morals, carriage and address of his pupils, he doubts not but the people of this state will cheerfully bestow on their children this polite and necessary part of their education."[38] Whether classes were mixed or separate usually depended on the number of pupils an area afforded, which meant that in most Connecticut towns boys and girls learned together. But masters were always willing to give private instruction to anyone who felt embarrassed by the presence of the opposite sex.

In New York city the larger population and interest in dancing easily supported several dancing masters who offered classes for both boys and girls and even for different age groups. There was opportunity aplenty for mixed dancing at assemblies which the masters sponsored and at balls organized as subscription-series by private groups. Art lessons were in sufficient demand to warrant the establishment of the Columbian Academy of Painting in 1792 and the New-York Academy of Fine Arts in 1802. The great thirst for music lessons prompted the following newspaper comment in September of 1801.[39] "With respect to music, the rage for it is so strong, that I dare not give my opinion fully on the subject. I would advise the ladies, however, not to

38. *Connecticut Courant*, Jan. 28, 1799.
39. *The Spectator*, Sept. 26, 1801.

value themselves too highly on their skill in this art, as, after their utmost pains, we can hire superior artists to play for us for a few shillings," and even a highly accomplished lady generally "will suffer the harpsichord to go out of tune after marriage."

The writer was equally concerned about the current craze for dancing and drawing because, in his opinion, the main subjects in female education should be literary and domestic, in order to make women rational companions, good wives, and good mothers. To paint a flower, to strum on an instrument, and to execute some difficult maneuvers in dancing were pleasing talents, to be sure, but not when "suffered to trespass too much on more important occupations." Lessons in deportment were of little value, he thought, for if a girl "is so fortunate as to live under the inspection of a discreet and well educated mother, even her manners will discover the modest decorum and bewitching grace, which no master can teach, and without which, female beauty is vulgar and female knowledge disgusting." His criticisms, in sum, were that modern female education sacrificed the useful to the ornamental; it bred artificiality of behavior; and it encouraged young ladies "to copy servilely all the extravagancies of dress which the caprice of fashion may prompt." He was not the only moralist writing on the subject in 1801. Another newspaper letter assigned the blame for these deplorable tendencies to the men who, when any lady was mentioned, asked "not whether her mind be enlightened, or her conversation intellectual, but if she sings, dances and dresses with taste."[40]

The moralistic observations about education that were printed in New York during 1801 have such a distinct New England flavor that they may well be another example of Connecticut influence in the city press, contributions perhaps from Noah Webster, a Connecticut man who had un-

40. *Ibid.*, Jan. 21, 1801.

til recently been editor of *The Spectator*, the paper in which the letters appeared. The Puritan heritage of modesty, thrift, and diligence still survived in Connecticut accompanied by a belief that the pernicious influence of the English had long been undermining these virtues throughout America,[41] and with special success wherever Englishmen were concentrated, as they were in New York.

This particular anti-English prejudice was part of Connecticut's distrust of New York and part of Mrs. Trumbull's obvious aversion to the high-living family of John Barker Church who had recently come from England. It can be detected also in a letter which Governor Trumbull received from his brother. John Trumbull, who took a bride in England about this time, wrote caustically of the education of women in England and described the sensible training to diligence and thrift that his wife had received. "The education of Mrs. T." he said, "I am happy was not of the fashionable kind."[42] And was it Connecticut prejudice that made *The Spectator*, as part of its little reform campaign, publish a letter on English female education extracted from a London print? Its readers would have had no difficulty in seeing that education in America was being distressingly reoriented to resemble the English pattern. The author, after caricaturing the overemphasis on beauty care and dancing in a young lady's training, went on to say:

> She is now equipped for the world, and sets out to see company, but she is first informed that she must beware of reservedness, and fence against a blush; for these are country vices, symptoms of vulgar rusticity; crimes against good breeding, and should

41. Morgan, *The Gentle Puritan*, pp. 264–65.

42. John Trumbull to Jonathan Trumbull, London, May 1, 1801, in Theodore Sizer, ed., *The Autobiography of Col. John Trumbull* (New Haven, 1953), p. 353. A fashionable education was precisely what John Trumbull's nieces were acquiring in New York. The artist, who had been in England for several years was apparently unaware of how rapidly ideas about female education were changing in Connecticut.

be carefully avoided. She is therefore taught a qualifying embellishment, in the fashionable world called *Assurance;* in the Christian, *Confidence;* and thus she mortgages modesty for behaviour, and almost robs the woman to equip the lady.[43]

Whatever the lessons of New York society, Harriet Trumbull never lost her "reservedness"; and it is not likely that either she or Maria was educated into extravagance of dress because, a few years after their visit to the city, it was reported in Connecticut that the independent Miss Trumbull kept wearing the same simple white gown to all the Hartford Assemblies, and that only someone in her social position would have dared do it.[44] The gown was probably one of those made for the girls in New York.

With the thought in mind of poor Mama back in Lebanon, worrying that her daughters were acquiring unbecoming city manners and tastes,[45] Harriet and Maria omitted from their letters some things that they knew would distress her. Probably because of Mrs. Trumbull's disapproval of playgoing, the letters say little about the girls' experience at the theater. Mrs. Trumbull was not alone in this prejudice. Though interest in dramatics had grown apace with interest in music, the theater had remained an unceasing subject of hostility in Connecticut. For years it was the exclusive realm of persistent amateurs such as the Yale undergraduates who from time to time attempted a play and thereby brought public opprobrium on the college. In a few towns the young people could occasionally prepare and present a performance or two without causing a stir; and students sometimes included historical dialogues, tableaux, and pantomimes in the public exhibitions at their college

43. *The Spectator*, Jan. 28, 1801.

44. J. Hammond Trumbull, ed., *The Memorial History of Hartford County* (Boston, 1886), I, p. 586.

45. The mother of Julia Cowles had the same worries when her daughter went off to Hartford and Middletown. *Diaries of Julia Cowles*, p. 25.

or school. But when traveling troupes of professional actors began to visit Connecticut in the 1790's and Hartford built a theater to accommodate them, public hostility rose so sharply that the state legislature in May 1800 enacted a law prohibiting professional theatrical performances of any kind whatsoever.[46]

Because of the scarcity of plays and the prejudice that surrounded them it is questionable whether Harriet and Maria Trumbull had ever seen a professional performance before going to New York. During their six months in the city they attended the new Park Theater six times. It had its own resident acting company, an orchestra, and an awesome array of scenery which William Dunlap, the manager, seems to have regarded as one of the theater's chief drawing cards, for he frequently included lengthy descriptions in his newspaper advertisements. On March 23 in *Peru Reveng'd*, for example, the girls saw recreations of the palace of Pizarro and the temple of the sun which were advertised as "displaying all the magnificence of Peruvian superstition." Dunlap, who was an artist as well as manager, conceived the temple with a breach in its wall made by an earthquake and with an altar upon which a sacrifice offered by the Inca could somehow be "consumed by fire from above." By causing a sun to rise above the cupola of the temple he differentiated morning from evening. On May 6, when Harriet and Maria attended *Le Deserteur de Naples* the newspapers promised "A View of a Village near Naples, a River and Cascade at a distance, Mountainous Country

46. Material on the drama (as well as on dancing, drawing, and music instruction) is widely scattered in Connecticut newspapers and town histories cited on other pages. See also Morgan, *The Gentle Puritan*, pp. 320, 364, 366; Trumbull, *History of Hartford County*, I, pp. 580–86; Mary E. Perkins, *Old Houses of Norwich* (Norwich, 1895), p. 347; and *Acts and Laws of the State of Connecticut in America* (Hartford, 1796), containing appendix with laws through May 1802, p. 521.

&c &c," also a scene of "Dark Night and a Snow-Storm"; but the climax of the play was obviously to be "A View of Mt. Vesuvius at the time of an eruption, with the Lava flowing." Theatrical companies sometimes used real water, fireworks, and other props to impress the customers, but whether in this particular scene Vesuvius actually belched fire is not clear.

In their six evenings at the Park Theater the girls saw a wide variety of pieces, for each program was a double bill carefully balanced by Dunlap to attract an audience for the pit and gallery as well as for the boxes. The theater, which could seat about 2000 people, opened its doors at 5:30 P.M.; and at 6:30 the curtain rose on performances that ran the gamut of tragedy, comedy, farce, comic opera, pantomime, dancing, and music both instrumental and vocal. The girls even saw Dunlap's special attraction for the 1800–1801 season, M. Laurence, a French dancer who had recently been performing in the West Indies. M. Laurence claimed to have studied with Vestris, the famous ballet master, but New York audiences liked him none the more for that, and the drama critics were brutal. "Pray Mr. Manager," asked one, "where did you pick up this *celebrated pupil* of the *celebrated Vestris*? . . . To speak plainly once for all and be no more pestered with him, his steps are wanting in grace, agility, variety and correctness. It may pass for dancing in the West Indies, though we very much doubt it, but we desire to see no more of it here."[47] M. Laurence persevered however, and in April began to receive favorable notice. But one of the young actors, less brave than the Frenchman, forced the company to cancel its second performance of *Abbé de l'Epée* when he withdrew from his role because of a review which advised that "if the manager wishes to save the play from being damned at the next representation, he

47. *The Spectator*, Feb. 28, 1801. See also *New-York Gazette*, April 7 and 11, 1801.

has no way left but to new cast some of his parts so as to procure another *St. Alme*."[48]

Because of the cancellation Harriet and Maria missed seeing *Abbé de l'Epée*. It was just as well for Mama's peace of mind, because Theodore, the juvenile lead in the play, was performed by an actress, and such impersonation (also men playing female roles) was one of the principal grounds of prejudice against the theater in Connecticut. Benjamin Silliman (Harriet's future husband) after attending a London theater in 1805 had this to say on the subject:

> If a modest woman can so far overcome reluctance which she ought to feel to such an indecorum, as to appear on a public stage in masculine attire, she must at least belong to that class of virtuous women whom Addison calls Salamanders. She is, in the language of this acute discerner of human characters; "a kind of heroine in chastity, that treads upon fire, and lives in the midst of flames without being hurt."

But perhaps even Silliman could have agreed with the New York critics about the purity and restraint with which the actress Mrs. Powell portrayed her male role in *Abbé de l'Epée*. Young Theodore was both deaf and dumb.[49]

It has always been difficult for actors to please everybody in their audience. Few are great enough not to bore one man or offend another. In New York, as elsewhere then and now, it was the ladies who took most offense, and so we find that in the decade surrounding 1800 young men commonly attended the theater together and husbands sometimes went without their wives.[50] According to one drama lover, some of the New York ladies even conducted a boycott of sorts, and he appealed to them to "make it a point to fix upon

48. *Ibid.*, March 11, 1801.

49. Benjamin Silliman, *A Journal of Travels in England, Holland, and Scotland in the Years 1805 and 1806* (New York, 1810), I, p. 195.

50. Diaries of Elizabeth Bleeker and John Anderson Jr. (1794–1798, manuscript in New-York Historical Society).

such evenings for *giving their parties,* as would not interfere with our theatre, and lend their countenance once more to make it fashionable to appear in the Boxes."[51] The manager tried to lure more ladies into his theater by urging the men to discontinue smoking "segars" there and by cleaning up some of the playwrights' language. But in spite of William Dunlap's corrections and erasures one critic thought the ladies still justified in staying away because

> there are suffered to remain many expressions in the plays which offend every modest ear, and which if addressed to or uttered in the presence of any woman of reputation in any other place [*than the theater*], would be considered as an insult and outrage, and as fixing an indelible stain on her character, if not frowned upon [*by her*] with instant and open indignation. . . . Even where the ideas and language in a play are unexceptionable: still in the performance much impurity is found, supplied from the fruitful imaginations of the actors themselves, who are well skilled in the art of polluting by their manner even the chastest scenes and sentiments.[52]

Advocates of the theater of course took a different view of the situation and maintained that the theater, while charming the senses, could "improve the taste and amend the morals." This argument was a common one, used also to win support for the drama in Connecticut;[53] and it did carry some weight, since often the heroes and heroines in plays were superlatively principled creatures and plots were educational demonstrations either of virtue triumphant or of the sad but just wages of sin. But a typical Connecticut answer to these arguments by a man who thought he was making a liberal statement was that "the truth is, the theater is not a school for morals; it is idle to pretend any such thing; it is a splendid fascinating amusement to those who

51. *The Spectator*, Feb. 28, 1801.
52. *Daily Advertiser*, March 9, 1801.
53. See, for example, *Connecticut Courant*, August 5, 1799.

have no worse views in attending it, but to multitudes the theatrical entertainment is only a secondary object."[54]

Theater and lessons and mile after mile after mile of social calls eventually wearied Harriet and Maria, and they longed to be home again in quiet slow-paced Lebanon. The letters of other Connecticut visitors to New York, even adults who were there on business, reveal that they felt the same way about "that noisy tumultuous city."[55] Connecticut held a strong grip on the hearts and minds of her sons and daughters, and several of the Connecticut men mentioned in the girls' letters, after winning success in New York, finally returned to their native state.

For all their eagerness to be back in Connecticut, Harriet and Maria learned after they got home to think kindly again of New York. It gradually became apparent that the months in the city had weaned Maria from country life. She spent less and less time in Lebanon, staying instead with her married sister, Faith Wadsworth, in busy Hartford. In 1804 she returned to New York as the wife of Henry Hudson, her beau in these letters; but Hudson, a Connecticut man, had had enough of business in New York and in December they set up housekeeping in Hartford. Within a year Maria died, after giving birth to a son.

Once separated from the disquieting city environment, Harriet nursed pleasant recollections of good friends in New York, and she and Eliza Sebor began a lifelong correspondence. Eliza became an annual visitor at Lebanon, and in 1802 Harriet went again to New York. This time she stayed

54. Silliman, *Travels*, I, p. 195. See also Rachel Huntington's letter to her sisters in Norwich Conn. dated New York, Nov. 19, 1796 in William D. McCracken, ed., *The Huntington Letters* (New York, 1897), p. 116.

55. Grace Cogswell Root, ed., *Father and Daughter: A Collection of Cogswell Family Letters and Diaries, 1772–1830* (West Hartford, 1924), pp. 45, 47.

with the Sebors and felt happier. Yet Harriet's pleasures seem never to have been complete. She had a touch of her mother's melancholy and would forever feel not quite comfortable in any city or indeed any setting that kept her long from home. In a characteristic letter to Eliza some years later, she remembered how "unpleasantly I felt when visiting alone the winter I spent with you."[56]

Harriet traveled and visited much in the years that followed and did learn to face the world with the outward assurance that her trips to New York were designed to give her. In 1809 she married Professor Benjamin Silliman of Yale, the first American professional chemist, and to them were born twelve children, from whom Harriet could not hide the basic timidity of her nature. She revealed a good deal of herself when she confessed to them that she could never listen to her illustrious husband lecture without a fear that he might break down. Her season in New York had not really dispelled her anxieties, but perhaps it helped her to endure a good many seasons in New Haven.

56. Harriet Trumbull to Eliza Sebor, Feb. 19, 1807, Silliman Family Collection.

# Letters

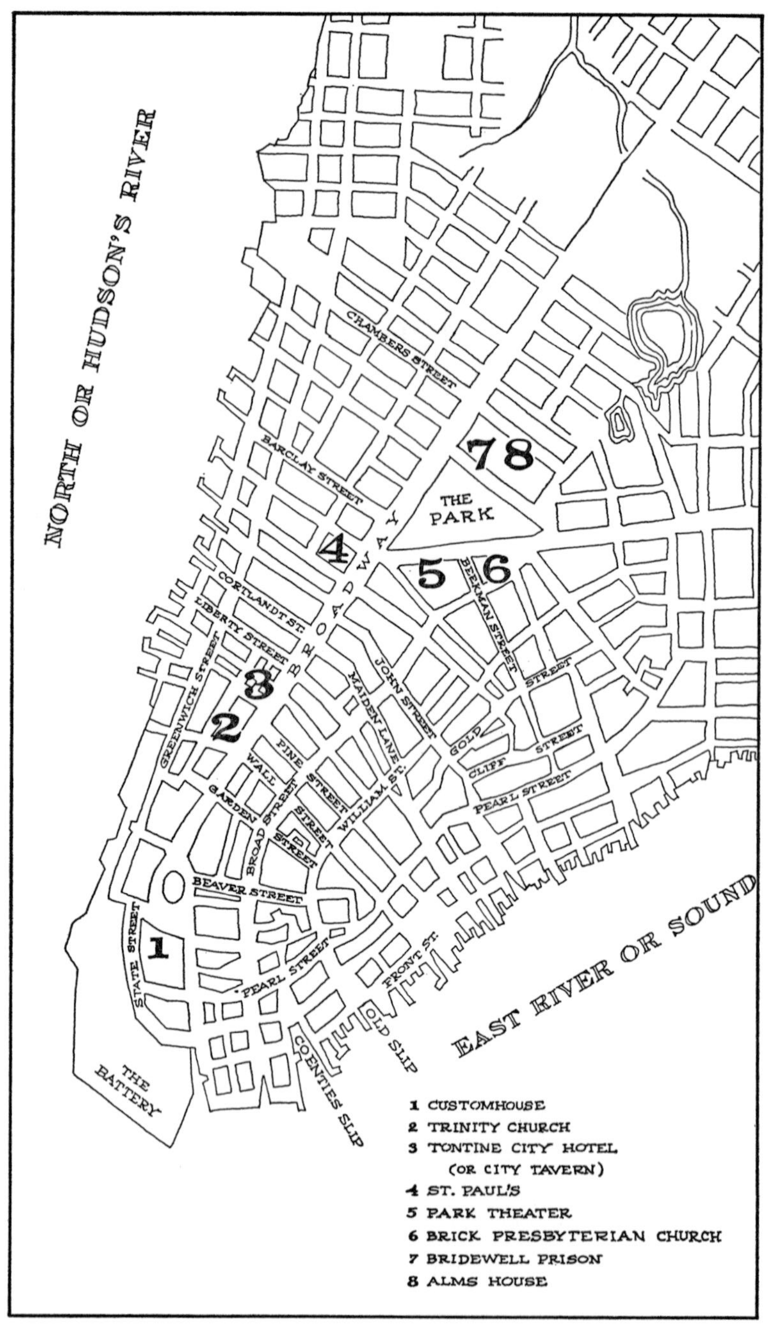


*New York in 1801, showing streets and places frequented by Harriet and Maria Trumbull.*

(Map based on the Taylor-Roberts plan, published in 1797.)

New Haven saturday eve [*November 29, 1800*]

DEAR PAPA

Here we are at Mr Butlers[1] all in good *trim*, and Harriet has quite got over her *heighpo*[2] and feels very well—we have had quite a pleasant ride—tho' the roads are not very good—Brother[3] seems to feel not much fatigued—he has gone out to see the folks about town—and we have not yet been to supper—tho we are in expectation of some *nice good* oysters—I wish Mama was here to eat some with us—pray dear Papa give my very best love to her—and to dear Sister—I have a very poor pen and you must excuse the badness of this writing—I shall leave it unsealed, 'till Brother comes in—perhaps he will wish to say one word, adieu, my dear Papa do keep up Mamas spirits as well as you can—she will hear from us every night. Your affectionate child

M TRUMBULL

*[written on back of preceding letter]*

MY DEAR FATHER

We *now have* been to supper, and are *still* very well, in spite of the good Oysters—Maria has said everything that is necessary respecting our journey.

1. The public house of Justus Butler on Church St. had a reputation for good food.
2. Hypochondria (p. 8); also referred to in these letters as "lowpo."
3. Daniel Wadsworth (1771–1849), brother-in-law of Harriet and Maria (husband of their sister Faith), was a Hartford merchant reputed in later life to be the wealthiest man in Connecticut.

The girls are in good spirits & health, & Brother *much* better than yesterday—Tell Faithy to send for some anodine balsum to doctor Hopkins' store. I intended to get some for her this morning but other cares drove it out of my head—tho' they were of much less consequence.

I think we are all doing very well in our journey, as well as in health & spirits—My best love to Mama & Faithy—& the Papas Mamas &c of the other houses. Your affectionate Son

DANIEL WADSWORTH

Please to Tell F*[aith]* that we shall wish to hear from home very often

*To Mrs. Trumbull at Hartford*

New York [*Tuesday*] December 2d [1800]

Dear Mama

Here we are at last, in *New York* both very well, and in very good spirits *considering all things*. We had a charming journey, and were fortunate enough to find very good company. I suppose you have heared two or three times from us since we left you—we wrote from New Haven and from Stratford[1]—I should have written the night before last—but Brother thought it was hardly worth while—as you had heared from us so little time before—and I believe he wrote himself yesterday—Harriet I think seems to be in better spirits than I expected—and behaves quite *bravely*.—Lady Kitty appears to be a very charming woman—and we begin to love her already—the young folks too—seem quite agreable and obliging—and we have got aquanted *considerably*—thier names—are Fanny, Sally, *Harriet*, and *Maria*—and the young gentlemen—John and William—we have each of us you see a namesake[2]—O and one other thing Mama (as you told me to be *very* particular) we really live very well—we had yesterday—roast turkey and boiled and broiled mutton—and to day, roast chickens and roast pork—so you see—we are in no danger of starving—we have been to day out a shopping—and have purchased some dark muslin—and some silk for petticoats and I have got some pocket handkerchiefs—we live in quite a pleasant street—tho' it is *quite* retired—[*they?*] have a very comfortable small brick house with two rooms which are furnished very

1. This letter is missing.

2. Henrietta Duer was apparently called Harriet. Although Catherine (b.1788) and Alexander (b.1793) Duer are not mentioned by name, several letters seem to refer to their presence in the household.

pretily—a [*torn*] and an entry—and our chamber is a very pleasant one—it is in the front of the house—and the furniture a large clever carpet, a bed with curtains (and very nice sheets) a sofa, some green chairs—a table, a wash stand, a large looking glass—and a picture—and there are three nice large closets—Lady Kitty has quite a large library—with many valuable books—among which is Rollins Ancient History[3]—so that Harriet will have an opportunity of finishing it—Lady Sterling (Lady Kitty's mother) seems to be a very good old lady indeed—the two young gentlemen—eat and sleep at home—they too *appear* very clever—the whole family treat one another with a *great deal of affection*. The eldest young ladys are abot as large as Harriet and myself—one of them is a very great romp, and the other quite sober, and serious—you see Mama I have been very particular, as you bade me. We have got a mantuamaker to make our gowns—and one thing Mama I must not forget—that is, that we have very good fires all the time—so that we *shant frieze* niether I hope, and now my dearest Mama I dont know that any thing remains to say only, that we love you and dear Papa dearly and want to see you very much, tho' we dont intend to be homesick *(if we can help it,)* pray give my best love to Sister, and remember us to all friends—adieu dearest Mama I remain with sincere gratitude and affection Your

MARIA TRUMBULL

3. *The Ancient History of the Egyptians, Carthaginians, Assyrians, Babylonians, Medes and Persians, Macedonians, and Grecians* by Charles Rollin (1661–1741), a Frenchman. During the eighteenth century numerous editions of from seven to twelve volumes were printed in English. The diary of Julia Cowles records her reading it in school in Connecticut at the age of twelve.

*To Mrs. Trumbull at Hartford*

New York [*Sunday*] December 7th 1800

[*no salutation*]

From this great bustling city, I sit down to address a few lines to my dear Mama, to inform her of health and happiness, the former (as usual) very good, and the latter as great as I could expect, when seperated from my best friends. Our journey here was very pleasant, and our present situation quite agreeable: Lady Caty is a very fine woman, and treats us with great kindness, as well as the other parts of family. As we talked about her age some time ago, I have the power to satisfy your curiosity, as I heard her mention she was forty five. We have as yet been out but once, and that, to Mr Watsons,[1] they treat us with great attention and we feel ourselves much obliged by their politeness, tomorrow we dine at Mr Churches,[2] which I regret extremely, for I hoped they

1. James Watson (1750–1806), merchant, had moved to New York from Hartford by 1786. In March 1800 he resigned from the U.S. Senate in order to accept appointment from President Adams as Naval Officer of New York City. During the period when these letters were written he was the Federalist candidate for lieutenant governor and under attack by the Republican press. He lost the election and was dismissed from the naval office by President Jefferson. [6 State St.]

2. John Barker Church (1748–1808) was an English adventurer who came to America at the beginning of the Revolution to see what profit could be made out of the war. Under an assumed name, he spent several lucrative years dealing in army supplies for the rebel forces. After the peace he returned to England with a wealthy American wife. He became a member of Parliament and one of the gay-living, extravagant "Carlton House set" (friends of the Prince of Wales) among whom, according to one source, manners were always superior to morals. In 1797 he moved to New York, made 52 Broadway his home, and was soon known as the city's most lavish host, entertaining daily, it was said, with plates of silver. He was one of the perpetrators of the fraudulent Manhattan Water Company (actually

would have taken no notice of us, brother is going to stay one day longer, to accompany us, which will make it more supportable. We have not began any of our studies but brother has arranged every thing with our masters and this week we are to begin with them: our dear Brother has taken a great deal of pains and trouble to settle every thing to our satisfaction and has succeeded, we owe him a great many thanks for all his goodness; he has also procured the ring you wish'd for, and I hope pleasing to you.

Maria this day received a letter from Sister, and we are happy to hear that you my dear Mama are better, I hope your health will continue to mend till it is quite good. Do my dear Mama stay at Hartford as long as you can, for I am sure that both you and Sister will be happier while you do; I shall often this winter wish to be with you by our own good fireside at Lebanon, but I beg you will feel no anxiety on our account, as we shall I think be quite contented, and will endeavour to behave as you would wish, and the time allotted for our absence will soon slip

---

a new banking corporation put over on the public by trickery) which was supposed to supply the city of New York with clean country water but did not. The Trumbulls' obvious aversion to the Churches arose not only from distrust of their principles and dislike of their conspicuous consumption but also, perhaps, from some feeling of family humiliation: John Trumbull, the governor's brother, while residing in England had for several years been heavily in debt to Church, whose aid helped the young artist to continue his studies. In spite of their expressed antipathy toward the Churches, the letters of Harriet and Maria Trumbull cannot hide their unwilling fascination and yearning for acceptance by this prestigious family. Harriet, we hope, was satisfied some years later when her daughter Maria Trumbull Silliman married the grandson and namesake of John Barker Church.

away. Brother will be able to tell you every thing about us more particularly than I can write, I fear our expenses will be greater than Papa expected, but when he thinks his money runs too fast, he has only to recall us. Dear Mama I hope you will as well as Papa write to us as often as possible, as your letters will always give us the greatest pleasure. Adieu dear Mama give my best love to dear Papa, and I beg you both to believe me your grateful and affectionate Daughter

HARRIET TRUMBULL

*To Governor and Mrs. Trumbull at Hartford*

[*New York*] Sunday evening December 7th [*1800*]

MY DEAR PAPA & MAMA

Altho Harriet has written you a long letter yet I thought as *there was so good an opportunity* you might prehaps be pleased to recieve a word or two from me too—we have to day received a letter from Sister informing us that Mama still continues better and that the old croocked doctor[1] is *driveing* off the *heighpo* as fast as he can—I can assure you we are not without *some* hopes of seeing you both in *New York* this winter my dear Papa and Mama—it would really be quite funny were you to come and have Miss *Lydia Robinson*[2] to accompany you, we have not seen Welthy[3] yet for all we have been in town almost a week—she has called once or twice but not found us—we expect to go and see her tomorrow—Mr Little[4] has just been in to see us and invite us to his house—and tomorrow Oh dear! we have got to dine at Mr Churchs! to my very great consternation and dismay!—however as we dont go untill 4 oclock that comforts me a *little*—and I hope to get dinner over—without committing any *unpardonable* error—and then to return home with all "possible precipitation"— — —Mrs

1. Dr. Lemuel Hopkins (1750–1801), physician, poet, satirical and political writer (p. 25, n. 28), was one of the group of literary intellectuals known as the Hartford Wits. His posture was apparently very stooped.

2. (1757–1825). Lebanon spinster, daughter of Ichabod Robinson (p. 122, n. 7).

3. Weltha Morgan (1784–1845), daughter of John Morgan, a Hartford merchant and banker.

4. Jonathan Little (b.1756), formerly of Lebanon, was doing business in New York by 1787. [10 John St.]

Woolsey sent for us on thursday but we did not go—we were at Mr Watsons on friday and accompanied them to the play[5] in the evening—but I am scribling away all so fast and most probably Harriet has told you all before and as I have three other letters to write this evening I believe I will bid my dearest Parents good night—I cant say but (were I to indulge it) I should be a little homesick some times but I intend to [*be*] contented if possible tho I almost think some times that I should like to run home with brother for a few minutes at least—adieu my dear dear Papa & Mama do let us hear often from you and believe me with the sencerest gratitude your truly affectionate daughter

MARIA TRUMBULL

5. The girls saw "the celebrated comedy of Catherine & Petruchio" and a comic opera, *The Spanish Castle* or *The Kinghts of Guadalquiver* with music composed by Harriet's piano teacher, James Hewitt. This was the first performance of *The Spanish Castle* and it was received, said the next day's review, "with that uncommon warmth of approbation which marks it as the popular piece of the season." The premier had been advertised for the previous Wednesday, but a tragedy had been substituted because of the death of an infant of one of the performers. *Commercial Advertiser*, Dec. 3 and 6, 1801.

*To Governor Trumbull at Hartford*

New York [*Thursday*] December 11th 1800

MY DEAR PAPA

I return you a thousand thanks for your dear good letter, which I received quite *unexpectedly* the morning that Brother left us, for I had not even thought of hearing again so soon, but it was a great deal better for that. I suppose this evening you will have the pleasure of seeing Brother, and hearing I hope a satisfactory account from us;[1] we felt so dismally the morning he went from here that we never once thank'd him for his goodness to us, but I *think* he will not impute it to ingratitude or want of sensibility to his kindness, and I beg you dear Papa to assure him how much we feel endebted to him. I am very glad to hear that Mama is better, and wish she could be persuaded to continue at Hartford some time longer, as I am convinced she will enjoy herself much more, than at Lebanon so much alone; but I fear she will think her presence cannot be longer dispensed with at home: I beg that neither she nor you Papa will feel any anxiety on our account, as I trust we shall be very safe, and I hope good. We went on Tuesday to drawing school, and were very well pleased with our instructors:[2] yesterday morning we walked down to Mrs. Watsons, they appeared glad to see us, and desired us to come there very often; we dined and spent the rest of the day at Mrs Woolsey's,[3] with

1. Harriet apparently expected Daniel to describe the dreaded dinner at Mr. Church's on Monday, for her journal covers every day but this.

2. The brothers Archibald and Alexander Robertson had arrived from Scotland about ten years earlier, and in 1792 opened the Columbian Academy of Painting. [79 Liberty St.]

3. The former Abigail Howland (1776–1833) of Norwich, now mar-

Weltha Morgan and Betsey Howland;[4] in the afternoon Mrs Coit[5] Mrs Leffingwell,[6] Miss Beers & Miss Sherman from New Haven, a daughter of the late General Williams,[7] Mr Jesse Brown,[8] and one or two other ladies and gentle men were there, we had quite a collection of Connecticut people. Most of them went to the play in the evening, and urged us very much to go with them, but we refused; both Mrs. Woolsey and Mrs Coit treated us very kindly indeed, Mrs Woolsey said she was once your child, and now we should be her children. Perhaps you will

---

ried to George Muirson Woolsey (1772–1851), merchant, who had also grown up in Connecticut (p. 119, n. 3). [32 Greenwich St.] The puzzling second mention of Mrs. Woolsey in this letter refers to her girlhood visits in the Trumbull family.

4. Elizabeth Burt Howland (1782–1857), Mrs. Woolsey's younger sister who was visiting New York from Norwich.

5. The former Lydia Howland (1773–1852), older sister of Mrs. Woolsey, the wife of Levi Coit (1770–1850), merchant from Norwich who had moved to New York about 1798. [33 Greenwich St.]

6. The former Sally Maria Beers (1765–1830) of New Haven, wife of William Leffingwell (1765–1834) of Norwich, who moved to New York about 1793 (p. 87, n. 3). [44 Wall St.] Leffingwell's heavy losses from shipping seizures during the 1790's led him in 1800 to give up commerce and become a broker of stocks and insurance. He retired to New Haven in 1809 and was for many years that city's wealthiest inhabitant.

7. Joseph Williams, Norwich merchant and brigadier general in the Connecticut militia, died in October 1800, leaving ten children. Fifteen-year-old Sally came to New York to live in the family of Levi Coit (see note 5), her mother's brother. Coit later helped Sally's brothers to a start in business.

8. Jesse Brown, Jr. of Norwich, was about to enter into partnership with Joseph Howland and Joseph, Jr., father and brother of Betsy Howland, Lydia Howland Coit, and Abigail Howland Woolsey. The Howlands were preparing to move from Norwich (p. 123, n. 1) and Brown was to be the Connecticut anchor man of the firm which lasted until 1806.

laugh Papa at my giving you such a journal, but you remember Mama wished us to write very particularly all we should see and do. Mr Jonathan Little call'd to see us the other evening, and said his wife would have come with him but had a bad cold, he invited us to come to his house whenever we could. We have not seen Uncle Backus, nor Mr Lanman. I have not written to Uncle John[9] yet, and dont know as I shall, for I dont know what to write him, it seems hardly worth while to give him the trouble of sending out a piano forte, when perhaps we can get one as good and as cheap here. Mr Phelps[10] has just been here and urged us very much to go to the play tomorrow evening with him and Mrs Phelps, but for several reasons I thought it not best and had to maintain quite a dispute with him. I came of [*off*] victorious however, and had the pleasure to find Lady Kitty of my opinion. I fear he will think me rather obstinate. I have seen Miss Nany Brown twice, she inquired after you Papa, and desired (in which she was joined by Lady Kitty) that I would always remember her to you when I wrote. Please to make my very best love to dear Mama, Sister and Brother and believe me dear Papa your grateful and affectionate daughter

HARRIET

9. Uncle John Trumbull had gone to England in 1794 as secretary to John Jay on the latter's mission to negotiate a treaty. He had remained abroad and in 1796 was appointed to the Jay Commission as agent for the relief and recovery of American seamen who had been forced into service in the British navy. Harriet might have found Uncle John an unsympathetic purchasing-agent for, in his opinion, learning to play the piano was "a waste of time & trouble." John Trumbull to Jonathan Trumbull, London, May 1, 1801.

10. Timothy Phelps (1757–1812), a New Haven merchant, was at this time visiting New York and later moved there (p. 72, n. 7).

*To Governor Trumbull at Lebanon*

New York [*Sunday*] 14th December 1800

My Dear Papa

It was with great pleasure I can assure you that I recieved your very kind letter, it is the first time you have written me since I left you, altho I have written to you two or three times, I almost dispair of our ever recieving a letter from Mama,[1] I am sure she might spend a little time to write to her children some times at least, I hope however that it is not because she does not love us, or has *forgotten* us— — —we have just been interrupted by the entrance of Uncle Backus,[2] who has called for the first time since we have been here, he desires to be particularly remembered to all the Lebanon friends, he is a strange man as ever I saw—I should think he had just this minute come out of a band box— — —again I am interrupted—all the bells are ringing for fire and the children are frightened almost to death, Lady Kitty and William are gone out, and there is no man in the house, however you know Papa *nothing disturbs my composure*, and so here I am left almost entirely bymesf [*by myself*]—to write to you—it is a very lucky circumstance for me as it is quite still now and I can write in comfort. I believe I gave

1. Mrs. Trumbull sometimes found correspondence difficult. One of her later letters trails off incoherently with "I can neither write or think believe your very affection—." It is continued by Governor Trumbull who explains "Mama is so much out of humour with her letter and herself that she leave me to finish." Feb. 13, 1805 to Faith Wadsworth, Silliman Family Collection.

2. Christopher Backus (b.1754), Mrs. Trumbull's half-brother (born to her father's third wife), moved to New York in 1783. To judge by his periodic letters to David Trumbull requesting money, he was not a successful businessman. Trumbull Papers, Connecticut Historical Society.

Sister a journal of the week untill thursday evening—Roswell Colt[3] came to see us and gave us an invitation to go to the anacreontic concert, Mr Phelps also called and urged us very much to go to the play the next evening—however we were such good girls as to refuse, altho Lady Kitty thought it would be a very good opportunity and Mr Phelps would hardly take no, for an answer—but we really thought that it would be better for us to stay at home and not go to too many plays as it would take of [*off*] our attention from things of more consequence— —the fire encreases and I am almost afraid to stay alone myself—but here they come again, one of them crying dreadfully—there is no man in the house and they are very much afraid—but I am determined to keep up *my* courage—on friday there was a dreadfull storm[4]—and we did not go out—saturday we stayed at home all the morning—in the afternoon we went to drawing school—and Papa you cant

3. Roswell Colt (1779–1856) lived in Hartford until 1793, when the family moved to New Jersey where his father (Peter Colt, treasurer of the state of Connecticut) was to take charge of the affairs of the "Society for Establishing Useful Manufactures." This corporation (among whose promoters had been William Duer) was establishing an industrial community at Paterson. The enterprise collapsed in 1797 and the Colts moved to upstate New York. In 1801 Roswell was working his way up the commercial ladder in New York City. After achieving success there, he eventually rejoined his father and brother in Paterson, where the family had gained a controlling interest in the moribund manufacturing society and was beginning to play a significant role in the industrial development of New Jersey.

4. *The Gazette* reported that hardly a ship in the port escaped damage: "several dragged their anchors & went foul of others—some went on shore—and eleven sloops and small schooners sank at the wharves, some of which were deeply laden with grain, brick etc."

think how I get praised—I am really very much pleased
to think I succeed so much better than I expected—to day
we have been to Church all day—and tell Mama that
I have read two excellent sermons beside—Mrs Fay and
Mr & Mrs Seber have called to see us—we are to spend
tomorrow with the latter, and Wedensday with the
former,—Lady Kitty has got a great many very good
books—and I have begun to read Guthries universal
Geography—and I intend to begin the History of England,[5]
Harriet has found good Mr Rollin—and we have got
quite settled and I begin to feel so hungry that I can hardly
satisfy myself with eating—we live extremely well,
have excellent dinners—and buckwheat cakes plenty for
breakfast every morning—we have toast for tea, the butter
is not very good but I begin to like it pretty well—we
have just learnt where the fire was[6]—there are six store
burnt, but it is out now— Papa we are really a little home-

5. These works by William Guthrie (1708–1770) and David Hume (1711–1776) were, like Rollin's volumes on ancient history, standard reading for any well-educated young man and they had doubtless been used by the Duer sons. The geography was generally printed in two volumes, the history in six, eight, or twelve, sometimes including T.G. Smollett's extension of Hume's *History* from 1688 to 1783. Although widely read, the *History* was somewhat suspect because of its Tory bias.

6. Later reports indicate that the fire consumed a block of eight buildings (houses with shop fronts) on Front St. between Old Slip and Coenties Slip and that "during the conflagration, the ship Orion, laying in the harbor, was several times on fire, and was preserved only by being hurried into the stream." The fact that the fire, which raged for two hours, did not spread more disastrously was credited to the efficiency of two new fire engines just arrived from England (p. 115, n. 7). *Mercantile Advertiser* Dec. 15, 1800; and diary of Henry Laight, manuscript in New-York Historical Society.

sick now and then, but however we make shift to get over it some how or other—Mama would I am sure be allmost frightened did she know how very industrious we have grown of late, I declare I hardly ever did as much work in so short a time in my life before—we live in a back room[7] where we see no passing—and having no bodys house to run in and out of (you know Papa there are a great many in Lebanon) we dont know what to do with ourselves unless we are *doing something*—and have of course hardly been idle a minute—My Dear Papa I am really afraid that you wont be able to read all this, but I can not write well with out lines—pray give my very best love to dear Mama—I hope she will write before long—my love likewise to Aunt Nabby Hyde[8]—to Sally—and Thomas—and in short to every one who will take the trouble to enquire after me—Harriet joins me in all—do dear Papa keep Mamas spirits up as much as possible —I suppose you have all got back to Lebanon again—but I hope you wont think of settling down there for all the winter, do go to Hartford often and partake of *all* the *amusements*—adieu dearest Papa I remain as ever your very grateful and affectionate Daughter

MARIA TRUMBULL

7. Life in winter was confined to the rooms in which fires were kept burning. The girls' chamber in the front of the house was apparently not one of them.

8. Abigail Hyde (1744–1830), a Lebanon spinster, spent much of her life in the Trumbull household as housekeeper and one of the family.

*To Governor and Mrs. Trumbull at Lebanon*

New York [*Wednesday*] December 17th 1800

MY DEAR PAPA & MAMA

As your letter was in partnership, so I suppose mine may be too, we were very happy at last to get a line or two from Mama—I hope now the ice is broken and you have found that you *can* write Dear Mama that you wont let it be so long before we hear from you again—I suppose you have hardly recieved my last letter yet —I did not think untill I had done it, that by writing on sunday evening you would not get it at Lebanon untill the next week—so of course it must be very old—on monday we spent the day at Mr Sebers[1] and had a charming visit— they are really very clever people and treat us with a great deal of kindness and attention and with no ceremony— which I am very glad of, they wish us to come and see them very often and to do just as we would at home and Mrs Seber begs us to ask your permission for us to dine with them every sunday—They always go to Church in the afternoon and I really think that we shant be able to do that very often if we dine at home, for we dont get our dinner *very* early—seldom get thro' before three o'clock or *after*—tho we made out to get to Church twice last sunday—I hope you will be willing—for I am sure we shall be very happy there,—but to proceed, in the afternoon we went to see where the fire had been the night before, it still continued burning and really looked dreadfully—

1. Jacob Sebor (1755–1847), merchant, formerly of Middletown and New London, moved to New York about 1791 to take over the business of his brother who had just died. [51 Beaver St.] He returned to Middletown in 1806, following financial reverses.

tuesday morning Mrs Watson and Maria[2] called and took us to ride—and by the bye we are to spend the day with them every friday—we had a charming ride and returned just time enough to get our dinner and go to drawing school —and O Papa Miss Nanny Brown[3] dined with us—she

2. Maria Watson (1782–1851), daughter of John Watson of Hartford. After he died in 1795 she was educated in the family of her uncle James Watson in New York.

3. The relatives and acquaintances of Miss Ann Brown (b.1754) exemplify the interconnections of the colonial upper class. She was a daughter of William Browne of Salem, Mass. and his second wife, Mary French, a New Jersey relative of his first wife who had been Mary Burnet, daughter of William Burnet (royal governor first of New York and New Jersey and then of Massachusetts and New Hampshire) and Mary Van Horne of New York. Ann Brown, through her Van Horne—French connections, was related to the Clarkson, Livingston, and Alexander families of New York and New Jersey; and after being orphaned at an early age she and her younger sister Sarah were sent from Salem to New York to live with their Van Horne and Clarkson aunts. The social environment in which they grew up was not unlike that described in the Trumbull girls' letters. The sociability and interfamily visiting that took place among the Duer children and their cousins in 1801 was a continuation of the pattern which Nanny Brown, Kitty Alexander, and their cousins had lived through thirty years earlier. Even the Revolution had not completely stopped family sociability. With military passes, Lady Kitty had been able to visit in New York while it was occupied by the British; and the Brown, Clarkson, and Van Horne cousins apparently visited their relatives in unoccupied New Jersey (William Livingston, the governor, was their uncle, and Lady Kitty lived there also). It is probable that young Miss Brown first met Jonathan Trumbull during the war years and that she, in retrospect, romanticized the attentions of the gallant officer who was fourteen years her senior and already married. In 1789 they met again when Trumbull came to New York to represent Connecticut in Congress. During that same winter Nanny Brown renewed her friendship with Martha and George Washington. She had stayed with them for several days in 1773, in company with her much older half-brother, William Burnet Brown

talks much about you—and says she believes you *was in love with her once*, she really *beats* all the Old Maids that ever I saw—even Aunt Nabby Hyde—for a wonder—at drawing school we got highly praised—we drank tea at Lady Mary Watts's,[4] and returned home in the evening when we had a fine frolic, as indeed we do very often—so many girls and boys of us we dont often want for *fun*. I eat so much toast and beef and pork that I have been as stupid as a woodchuck all day—this morning—we were going out with Lady Kitty—but company kept coming in one after another so fast that I really did not know as we ever should go, however Mrs Seber called very soon—and as we were going to Mrs Fays to dine, we dressed us and went to walk with her, we went to a great many shops to look for bonnets which we really want very much—and saw *some* very pretty ones, I think we shall get some

---

(the Brownes gradually dropped the "e" from their name). William had moved to Virginia from Salem a few years after marrying Judith Walker Carter, a Virginia belle. Miss Brown and the Washingtons doubtless saw one another also during the Revolution—perhaps at Governor Livingston's house or at General (Lord Stirling) Alexander's. The Trumbull girls' correspondence mentions Nanny Brown as late as 1807, and she was probably still in New York in 1809–1813 when the city directory lists a "Miss Ann Brown, spinster" on Partition St.

4. Lady Mary Alexander Watts (1749–1832?), sister of Lady Kitty, and wife of Robert Watts, merchant. [35 Pearl St.] Watts took no active part in the War for Independence, and was regarded as a Tory because he and his family remained in New York during the years when it was occupied by the British. Lord Howe, the commanding British general, permitted Lady Kitty and her mother to visit Lady Mary for several weeks in 1778 while Lord Stirling (General Alexander) and his American troops were encamped at nearby White Plains.

tomorrow, we went home with Mrs Seber—and as we did not know the way to Mr Fays she sent a *sweet* young gentleman to gallant us—I ant in love with him however Papa—though he is certainly the prettiest young man we have seen—but there are so many handsome men here that I dont care any thing about them, we had a charming good dinner and I was *proper* hungry—they all treated us very kindly and I should have liked Colonel Fay[5] very much if he was not such a democrat—and altho I dont very well understand what they are, yet I dont like them at all, but Papa I must not forget to tell you—Colonel Fay sends his *love* to you—Mrs Fay was sending hers to sister and he told us not to forget his to you—they say here that Mr Jefferson and Burr are certainly coming in President and Vice President[6] but I believe it is time for me to stop—adieu my dearest Papa and Mama, give my very best love to all friends not forgetting aunt Nabby Hyde Sally—

5. Col. Joseph Fay (1753–1803), after an active military and political career in Vermont, resigned his post as secretary to the governor and council in 1794 and moved to New York, where he was a lawyer and merchant. His move may have been prompted by his marriage in 1793 to a daughter of Samuel Broome, a New York and New Haven merchant (p. 72, n. 7). Both men were Republicans. [57 Pearl St.]

6. The outcome was by no means certain at this time. Jefferson and Burr received an equal number of electoral votes and (according to the election system of 1801) it therefore fell to the House of Representatives to determine which should be president. The Federalists might thwart the Republicans by choosing Burr (the Republican vice-presidential candidate) rather than Jefferson for the presidency. In February the House voted 36 times before achieving the necessary majority (see also p. 136, n. 1).

and Abby Trumbull[7] and indeed every body who thinks or cares any thing about your very gratefull and affectionate Daughter

MARIA TRUMBULL

Harriets best love to all

7. Sarah (1779–1839) and Abigail (1781–1861), daughters of Governor Trumbull's brother David and Mrs. Trumbull's half-sister Sarah (born to her father's third wife).

New York [*Thursday*] 25th December 1800

DEAR PAPA

We have just had the pleasure of receiving your letter of the 22d and are a thousand times obliged to you for it, we have heard from none of our friends since Saturday, which is the longest time we have ever been without a letter, and it makes us so happy to receive one. I was quite surprised to hear from Sister that you had returned to Lebanon and left Mama at Hartford, but I was very glad of it and hope she will remain there a long time, tho I often think of you dear Papa, in your lonely situation and wish I was with you; not that I am uneasy or homesick, for tho I would gladly return any day, yet I am quite pleased and contented, Lady Kitty is a charming woman, and we like her more and more every day. I thank you Papa for all the information your letter contains, some of it indeed is disagreeable and unexpected, poor old Mr Tiffanny is gone then, and Benjamin Elliott! I dare say Uncle Williams[1] family are much grieved to hear it; I am glad for Nathan Williams friend, that he has returned, and wish that Jacob had come with him; I am happy to hear that our sick neighbors have recovered, I have thought of them often: our poor little tabby is gone then, what a pity, but I hope Sally will find another as pretty by the time we get home, the old cat I dont care much about.

And now Papa I will tell you our news, all the little we have, last Week on Monday we dined at Mr Sebors, with

1. William Williams (1731–1811) of Lebanon; signer of the Declaration of Independence; husband of Mary Trumbull, Governor Trumbull's sister.

Mr B Winthrop[2] and his wife, he inquired after you, as does almost every body we see; Tuesday we drank tea at Lady Mary Watts, they are very rich and live very genteely, Wednesday we spent at Colo Fay's, I believe Maria wrote that he sent his *love* to you; Thursday we went to drawing school, and drank tea with Mrs Sebor. Mr & Mrs Corp[3] were there, the latter said she should call and see us; Friday we passed a very pleasant day at Mr Watsons, they had no other company, and as the evening was very disagreeable they sent us home in their carriage, pray tell Aunt Nabby that James[4] is a fine boy and Maria quite admires him; Saturday it rained, that we could not go to drawing school and were at home all day, Sunday was very pleasant, we went to church in the morning with the young ladies (they go to St Paul's) we dined at Mrs Sebors, and went with her in the afternoon to Trinity; Colo Varick[5] and his Lady call'd to see us while we were gone, and Mrs Benson sent her card; in the evening Mrs Church and Mrs Hamilton[6] condescended to call. Mr

2. Francis Bayard Winthrop (1754–1817), merchant, formerly of New London, was the brother of Mrs. Sebor (Elizabeth Winthrop). [29 Wall St.]

3. Samuel Corp was an English-born merchant who had come to New York shortly after the Revolution. [171 Pearl St.]

4. James Talcott Watson (c. 1789–1839), only child of James Watson, graduated from Columbia College in 1804.

5. Richard Varick (1753–1831), mayor of New York 1789–1801, was another casualty of the Republican sweep. [108 Broadway.]

6. Mrs. Alexander Hamilton and Mrs. John Barker Church were sisters (Elizabeth and Angelica Schuyler). The Hamiltons lived at 26 Broadway, the Churches at 52 Broadway.

Phelps and Miss Broome[7] came in. Monday we staid at home, Tuesday we went to drawing school, Wednesday we went out in the morning to return calls, we went first to Mrs Woolseys and Mrs Coits, then came home, and went again with Sally Duer, to see some young ladies who had call'd on us, and to the Mayors, to Mrs Hamiltons, and Mrs Churches, but as the two last Ladies were not at home we only left cards, Today has been a great day, we went to church in the morning, it was all decorated with evergreen bushes; Mrs Woolsey asked us to spend the day with her, but we were before engaged to Mrs Sebor, we have just returned from there, they are all extremely kind and obliging to us, and wish us [*to*] feel quite at home there; tomorrow we spend at Mr Watsons, they have engaged us to pass every Friday with them, and say when the walking is bad, or it rains they will send the carriage for us, they also are very good to us and we feel very happy there, Mr Watson has given us a right in the city Library, and permission to take any book that he has in his house. I hope we shall behave and improve as well as you could wish, and make the best of the good opportunity afforded us for instruction and improvement, we are very well pleased with our masters, and hope they are equally so with us, they *sometimes praise* us, but *never find fault* with us. We see our good friend Roswell very often, he is

7. Henrietta Broome of New Haven, sister of Mrs. Phelps (Jennet) and of Mrs. Fay (Elizabeth). After Jennet's death, Henrietta became the second Mrs. Phelps. They were daughters of Samuel Broome, a New York merchant who, during the British occupation of the city, carried on his business from New Haven and then settled there in 1784. He continued to maintain close social and commercial connections (through a partner) with New York.

very polite to us, and we are to go with him to the anacreontic Concert, the 6th of January. I have one grievance, that of not hearing any news, I never hear any but when I accidentally overhear gentlemen talking and that but seldom, I should know as much again of what is passing in the world, at Lebanon: People here say that Mr Jefferson is going to be President, and Mr Burr vice President (I am sure they are both *vicious* enough) but I want to know *your* opinion Papa, as I consider that *almost infallible.* We intend sending you soon an account of our expenses, and hope you will think we have not been extravagant yet, I think most of the articles have been much needed. I am glad Mama is so much better as to think of having her gown altered, I send a great deal of love to all our friends at Lebanon, to Uncle Trumbulls family, Uncle William's, Aunt Nabby Duttons,[8] Aunt Nabby Hydy and all our family, Miss Hannah, Miss Betty and every body else that inquires about us: Please to tell Cousins Sally and Abby, that velvet bonnets of all shapes and colours are fashionable, that cagliquo [*calico*] is very much worn, I have seen no gowns made very different from what they have, they make them very scant with a collar that does not meet and small lappels to turn over. Adieu dear Papa accept the best love and wishes of your gratefull and affectionate Daughter

HARRIET TRUMBULL

8. Mrs. Trumbull's half-sister, Abigail Backus (b. 1761), the youngest child of her father's third marriage. She married Hubbard Dutton in 1797 and lived in Lebanon.

Marias best love to dear Papa, and every body. Mr Lanman[9] called to see us and politely offered to forward any thing we might wish to send, Uncle Christopher has been to see us twice but we were out the last time, he desired to be remembered to all friends, we call'd at Mr Littles once this week but they were out.

9. Peter Lanman (1771–1854) and his father (same name) were in business in both Norwich and New York, the son handling the New York end.

*To Mrs. Trumbull at Hartford*

New York [*Friday*] 26th December 1800

MY DEAR MAMA

It is indeed a great while since you have recieved a letter from either of us, and I flatter myself that you will be quite rejoiced to get this, am I not very vain? but to begin my journal, on monday morning we went a shopping almost all over town, in the afternoon we stayed at home, tuesday morning we were also out all the morning, calling on *folks*, in the afternoon we went to drawing schooll and in the evening had the company of our dear good Roswell Colt, wednesday—we went every where allmost, to Mr Coits, Mr Woolseys General Hamiltons, Mr Churchs, Mr Varricks Mrs Livingstons, Mr Rutherfords,[1] and in short allmost every where—I went in the afternoon to drawing school with the young ladys, and in the evening we had fine fun in fixing for Christmas—thursday we went to church in the morning—and dined and spent the remainder of the day at Mr Sebors, and got some sweet Christmas kisses—to day we have spent at Mr Watsons and enjoyed ourselves very much, as indeed we always do there—we have been escorted home by Roswell, who is waiting below for my letter, so that I must be in a hurry for it is quite late—tomorrow we go to drawing school, and next day to Mr Sebors—and now I believe you have the whole history, Mama Harriet wants

1. Walter Rutherfurd, an uncle of Lady Kitty, and Mrs. Peter R. Livingston, widow of a cousin. The former had a granddaughter and the latter a daughter of appropriate age to be the unnamed young ladies whom Harriet mentioned visiting on this day with Sally Duer (see p. 72). The Rutherfurds lived at 219 Broadway. Mrs. Livingston and her daughter may have lived in the home of her married son Peter at 11 Broadway.

to know of you, and wishes you should ask Sister what she thinks we had better do about getting white gowns—we really want them considerably, tho for my part I shall be quite contented without them, as I think I want a calico more but we will do just as you think proper and wish you to write us in your next, Maria Watson desires her love to all the Hartford friends, adieu my dearest Mama do drive off the old heighpo and be as merry as you can, present my very best love and respects to my dearest friends. Harriet joins me, and believe me to be your very greatfull and affectionate Child

MARIA TRUMBULL

*To Governor Trumbull at Lebanon*

New York [*Friday*] 2d of January *1801*!

My Dear Papa

We were so negligent last night as to go to bed without writing to you, and so to make up for it I have risen this morning *before sunrise*, that I may have my letter ready for one of the young men to carry as he goes to his Office—I suppose *you* will like to hear a journal of our proceedings Dear Papa, as well as the Hartford folks—therefore I will give you one, last friday we spent the day very pleasantly at Mr Watsons, and were escorted home by Roswell Colt who spent the evening with us—after he was gone we had fine fun playing—*Tom come tickle me.*[1] Saturday was a very chill day, however we made out to get to drawing school in the afternoon. Sunday it rained very hard and of course we did not go to Church—Monday being a fine day, I took quite a long walck in the morning—and in the afternoon we all hands drank tea at Mr Rutherfords in the Broad Way—there was a very large party and in the evening we played a great many different plays—but I did not enjoy my self much—tuesday morning we were out making calls all the morning—and in the afternoon went to drawing school—wednesday we stayed at home—Mrs Fay Mrs Bradley, Miss Broome and Mrs

1. Probably a teen-age version of what one nineteenth-century American gamebook described under "certain games of very little girls." The accompanying rhyme was self-explanatory: "Old maid, old maid, you'll surely be / If you laugh or you smile while I tickle your knee." An English version (c.1854) was played in a circle, with each player in turn pinching the nose (and sometimes also the ears, chin, and cheeks) of the next one while trying to make him smile. Smilers had to pay a forfeit and redeem it at the end of the game by performing some mirth-provoking penance.

Corp—called to see us—Harriet took a short walk—
Thursday I went to Church in the morning, and afterwards
we both spent the day at Mr Woolseys—where we
enjoyed ourselves very much—we returned before tea, and
were very much pleased at finding letters from home, I
should like very much to se [*see*] Sir John Sinclairs letter,[2]
I think it must be quite a curiousity, but we seem I
think to be quite *familiar* with *Lords* and *Ladys*—I suppose
you have heared that Uncle John was married—it seems
to come so direct that I think there can not be much
doubt of its being true, I should like however to know my
new Aunts name. Give my best love if you please to
Cousin Abby—I thank her a thousand times for her letter
and intend answering it another time—perhaps I shall
*confide* it to the care of a certain gentleman who has been so
obligeing as to offer to take the care of letters or any
thing else—tell aunt Nabby Hyde that I sympathise with
her about the sausages—I sincerely hope she has succeeded
at last—I think if she had kept her meet [*meat*] till this

2. (1754–1835). Writer on finance and agriculture, member of Parliament 1780–1811. He was at this time proposing to sell in the United States a facsimile edition of letters that General Washington had written to him "on Agriculture and other Interesting Topics," the profit from which was to be devoted "to the creation of some suitable Monument to his Memory." Sinclair had requested Governor Trumbull "to ascertain how many Copies it will be proper to transmit to your Part of America." Trumbull sent his correspondence on the subject to President Timothy Dwight of Yale, who was going to New York, and asked him to see about getting subscribers for the volume there. Dwight turned the job over to a Mr. Woolsey (probably his brother-in-law William W. Woolsey). Dwight to Trumbull Feb. 11, 1801, Jonathan Trumbull, Jr. Papers, Connecticut Historical Society; Sinclair-Trumbull Correspondence, New-York Historical Society.

time she would not have had much difficulty in freezing it for it was *monstratious* cold here, whatever it may be at Lebanon—give my very best love to her and to all the rest of our good Lebanon friends—Uncle Williams's and Uncle Trumbull family in particular—Papa when ever you wish us to send you an account of our expences—will you be so good as to send us word—as we are ready at any time—I was quite grieved to hear of the death of poor little tabby, Sally must not mourn too much for her however—we are going to day to Mr Watsons and expect to be very happy—and now my dear Papa I think I have written you a pretty tolerabl letter, upon an empty stomach too, Harriets best love. Your affectionate Child

MARIA

PS—Uncle Backus comes to see us often—he desires to be particularly remembered to his Lebanon friends

*To Mrs. Trumbull at Hartford*

New York [*Wednesday*] January 7th 1801

My Dear Mama

Tho you have not given me the pleasure of receiving a letter from you this long time, yet as it is a good while since I have written to you, and I am in debt to none of my other friends, I will address this letter to you, and hope it will be so fortunate as to be answered. Since the last letter that Maria wrote, we have been pretty quiet at home, and as the weather & walking are very bad I hope we shall remain so a few days longer, for when we are out walking and visiting so much, we cant do any thing else, and I am quite vex'd to think how little work I have done; when we first came, for two or three days I had no work, and began to work a cap crown for Aunt Nabby Hyde, I did about half of it, since when it has lain by and I dont know when it will get finished, for with my music and drawing, writing letters dressing and going out, my time is compleatly fill'd up, and I have no time even for reading. We had the pleasure of recieving letters from Hartford on Sunday, and hearing an account of our friends from Mr Hudsons own mouth, I am very happy to hear my dear Mama that your medicine does you good, and hope in a very short time you will be quite well; we have had some snow here and if (as I think is probable) you have had more, I imagine you have gone or will soon go from Hartford, I hope not as it will be so much duller at Lebanon, have you thought of what I mentioned, having Lydia Backus[1] to stay with you a few weeks? I dont doubt she would be very glad to, and she would be company for you: we are

1. Daughter of Ebenezer Backus, Mrs. Trumbull's brother. She lived in Norwich.

expecting to receive letters to day by Mr Morgan, Weltha will be very glad to see her Papa, I wish mine was coming too.

Last Friday we passed a very pleasant day at Mr Watsons, we went to ride in the morning and in the evening Roswell Colt was there and came home with us, Saturday it was dreadfull cold, but we went to drawing school without finding any ill effects from the weather, Sunday it snow'd all day and to our great disappointment prevented our going to church or to Mr Sebors, in the evening Roswell Colt and Henry Hudson[2] came in and brought us letters. Monday we staid at home, Lady Kitty had company in the afternoon. Tuesday morning Maria went to see Mrs Sebor, we had a hairdresser come to dress our heads for the concert in the evening, Roswell had presented Sally Duer Maria and myself with tickets, and Mr Lanman sent us two more to give to any one, as we had no occasion for them ourselves. Lady Kitty did not chuse to go, and I gave my ticket to Fanny, and Maria, hers, to John. In the evening we all went together to Mrs Woolseys as we were to go in company with her, Mrs Coit Miss Howland and Miss Williamson who is staying with Mrs Woolsey, the concert was in the city assembly room, it is a *very* large elegant room, and full of Ladies and Gentlemen all splendidly drest, I believe there were certainly 6 hundred Ladies, and a number very handsome and beautifully drest, we had some fine music and singing, a great many good things to eat, as cakes grapes almonds, &c a great deal of mirth and noise,

2. (b. 1780). The future husband of Maria. He was at this time a clerk in the firm of James Watson. (See also p. 109, n. 2.)

and came home between eleven and twelve O Clock.[3] Today we were to have gone to Mrs Sebors, but it rains and we stay at home to write letters to our friends. We received a very polite note from Mr & Mrs Varick requesting us to drink tea and pass the evening of Friday after next, with them, I suppose there will be a party, we returned for answer that we would do ourselves the honour to go. We see Uncle Backus often, he seems to know every thing about us and every one else, and is always drest very handsome and is neatness itself. Adieu dear Mama, please to give our best love to Brother and Sister, and all Hartford friends, Maria sends her best love to you, in which she is join'd by your very grateful and affectionate Daughter,

HARRIET T

3. The concert took place in the New City Tavern (also called the Tontine City Hotel) at 115 Broadway, between Thames St. and Cedar St. It was given by the Columbian Anacreontic Society, a sociable musical club that flourished for about five years at the turn of the century. Elizabeth Bleeker also attended the concert and recorded in her diary that she "was not much pleas'd with their choice of music."

*To Governor Trumbull at Lebanon*

New York [*Thursday*] January 8th 1801

My Dear Papa

After writing to you last friday—and carrying my letter to the post office[1]—we went to spend the day at Mr Watsons—and were really very happy—we went to ride with Mrs Watsons and Maria in the morning—and in the afternoon—we all set down to work, as we do at home—saturday it was colder it seems to me than ever it was before—I could hardly keep myself warm any how—for all I wore my spencer[2] almost all day—however notwithstanding it was so cold—we made out to go to drawing school in the afternoon. Sunday it snowed and we did not go to church—Lady Mary sent the coach for Lady Kitty and after she was gone the children to besure did make a most *royal* noise. However we made out to read several very good sermons—and I by *dint* of persuasion got away a novel from one of the young men—and gave him a sermon instead—and he really seemed so much pleased with it that I believe I shall try again next sunday—it was one of Blairs sermons to young people[3]—and I was sure he could not help likeing it—but he was quite in *raptures*. In the evening Roswell Colt and Henry Hudson called to see us, the latter brought letters from Hartford—monday we stayed at home all the day—in the afternoon Lady Kitty had

1. Corner of William St. and Garden St.

2. A snug, long-sleeved, waist-length (or shorter) jacket generally worn outdoors over a coat or dress. The diary of Henry Laight says that the temperature on this day was seven degrees at 3:00 P.M.

3. Dr. Hugh Blair (1718–1800), a Scottish clergyman and professor of rhetoric. His *Advice to Youth*, a collection of sermons on morality and the duties of the young, was printed in England and America in many editions.

company to tea—in the evening I read in the bible to Lady Stirling—and we went very early to bed—tuesday was the great day among the *gay* folks—in the morning I went to Mr Sebors—and after I returned did a thing which I never did before—and I was almost going to say never intend to again, it was to have my hair dressed by a *hair dresser*, and after he had done and I had paid him a *dollar*—it did not look half as well as it does when I only curl it a little myself—I positively felt ashamed. I looked so like a witch—and then it was so extravagant. Miss Brown dined with us—and she told me to tell you that she gave you a new years kiss, or rather she kissed your *picture*.[4] She is really very clever—tho' she has some *odditys*—at length came the long expected evening—and all in our best bibs and tuckers we set of [*off*] for the Anacreontic concert—it was in the city tavern, in a *monstrous* [*torn*] room—and there were upwards of six hundred people all most elegantly and splendidly dressed and they to be sure did make a *fine show*—we had every thing almost that was good to eat fruit nuts, and most *elegant* cake, however I did not enjoy myself very much, we returned about twelve oclock, wednesday it rained and we did not go out—Mr John

4. The picture of Jonathan Trumbull which Nanny Brown possessed could have been her own handiwork; but more likely it was drawn and presented to her by his artist-brother, John, either during the war years or during the winter of 1789, when he was in New York sketching portraits from which he later painted his famous historical scenes. He perhaps dashed off cartoons or cut silhouettes of the assembled company during some informal social evening that he and Jonathan and Nanny Brown spent together at the Duers' or at the Jays' (Mrs. John Jay was Nanny's cousin). It was common at the time for men and women of artistic bent to entertain their friends in this fashion.

Morgan called and brought us some letters—in the evening we sat up till after twelve playing *pope Joan*[5]—to day it has been raining—however we have been at drawing school and when we came home found a letter from you dearest Papa—for which we thank you ten thousand times. Uncle Backus has been to see us and has just gone—the young gentlemen have gone to a ball—Harriet and the young ladys are very quitly at work—and I as you have doubtless discovered ere now am writing to you—but I believe it is time to stop therefore with Harriets and my best love to all believe me your very grateful child

M Trumbull

5. A card game played with counters.

New York [*Saturday*] January 10th 1801

Dear Papa

Your letter was received as it should be on thursday and gave us a great deal of pleasure, as your letters, and those of our other friends always do, you are all very good to write so often, and we are quite proud of telling how frequently we hear from home, indeed we should very soon be homesick if we were to hear no oftener than Miss Morgan has. I think often of your lonely situation at Lebanon, but am very happy to hear that the neighbors are so kind, and hope they will continue their friendly visits when Mama returns, to whom I think they will be more necessary, as she will not be so interested in the Election of a President and other political affairs, as to divert her attention from loneliness of the situation. Dear Papa I wish when you come on to Hartford for Mama, that you would extend your journey to this city, it would make us *so very* happy, and then there are so many people here who would be glad to see you and whom you would be glad to see! Pray dear Papa think of it? I quite envied Weltha Morgan when her Papa came. We have had some snow but it is all gone; and some extreme cold, weather, one day in particular, Saturday, was wonderfull cold, 'twas hardly possible to keep warm any where; I believe our situation is colder than many in town, but not I imagine quite equal to Lebanon; we have much better fires than I was afraid we should from what was told us, indeed we have as good as any body need have. We have heard from Mr Pierpont[1] and Mr Lanman that Uncle John was married, I did not believe it at first, but Mr Lanman said [*he*] had

1. Hezekiah Beers Pierpont (1768–1838) moved from New Haven in 1790 and in 1793 entered into a commercial partnership with

letters in which it was mentioned, and that he had no doubt but it was true, he said he met an American gentleman in the street and asked him if he would go and see him made a *Benedick* of; the gentleman went and saw him married,[2] there was no other American present. He has taken a house in Hampstead of 250 pounds rent ayear, and lives in great style; Mr Lanman was not able to tell what the lady's name was;[3] there was a british packet arrived here a few day since, by which I hope you will receive letters giving some particulars.

Maria has written to you so lately Papa that I suppose she has told what we have been doing lately, and given you an account of the concert, and of our invitation to Mr Varick, we spent yesterday again at Mr Watsons, we are so happy there, that we dont want to leave them to come home; if we feel a little dull or uneasy we have only to take a walk there, sit an hour eat a piece of gingerbread, and return quite happy.

You are very good my dear Papa, to be so indulgent to us

---

William Leffingwell (p. 59, n. 6) that lasted until 1800. He was in France on business in 1794 (when he saw Robespierre beheaded) and again from 1797 until 1800, after the ship on which he was returning from China and India was seized by a French privateer and sold at Nantes for the equivalent of $330,000 American money. Pierpont remained abroad trying to recover damages from the French government and indemnity from an English insurance firm.

2. Christopher Gore, a college friend of Trumbull's and a fellow member of the Jay Commission.

3. John Trumbull married Sarah Hope Harvey (age 26) on October 1, 1800 and brought her to America in 1804. She soon became convinced that her husband's friends and relatives looked down on her family background and unfashionable domestic education (see p. 38, n. 42), and her unhappiness led to excessive behavior and drinking that scandalized and further alienated the Trumbull clan.

in letting us have new dresses and encouraging us to appear in a style suited to your station in life; money runs away so easily that we were almost afraid to get even necessary articles; I will enclose my account[4] of my expences since Brother left us, and of the money we have received from Mr Sebor; I hope you will think it moderate, tho I was almost frightened at it: we have purchased us some new dresses today, as we thought they were quite necessary—we dont wish to appear [*i.e. in the extravagant height of fashion*] as some of young ladies we meet with [do, but] to dress handsomely and so as your friends would not be asha[med of us]. I should like to see good old Lebanon, and eat some baked beans this evening—I feel very hungry and think of them very much just now! I hope all our friends and neighbors are well, is Doctor Clark married? or like to be?[5] and Papa have you got Simon with you yet, or Edmund? or who? If you are still at Lebanon, or when you go there be so good as to give my love to all our relations and friends, to Aunt Nabby Hyde and all our own family. Maria says give my best love to Papa, she is chatting away so that I beleive I must conclude by begging you dear Papa to beleive me your very grateful and affectionate Daughter

HARRIET TRUMBULL

4. A contemporary endorsement indicates that the enclosed account was for $32.

5. Dr. Thaddeus Clarke of Lebanon, whose father and three brothers were also doctors. Dr. Clarke was 30 years old and typical of the many men of his time who postponed marriage until they were well established in life. The above mentioned Mr. Pierpont and Mr. Lanman were 32 and 29 and also still bachelors; but all three men married within a year. John Trumbull remained single until he was 44, and Philip Livingston (p. 95, n. 5) until he was 50.

New York [*Wednesday*] 14th January 1801

My Dear Papa

Harriet has carried our Journal down to Saturday evening, and I will therefore take it up from sunday—which was very pleasant—we went to St Pauls in the morning—dined with Mrs Sebor, and went with her to Trinity in the afternoon—we spent almost all the evening at Mr Sebors, after which we returned, I read in the Bible to Lady Stirling, and we went pretty early to bed—Monday I was out almost all the morning—Mr Morgan and Mr Brunson[1] called to see us—the latter invited us to spend wednesday, (which is to day) with them —of course we are going. In the afternoon we went to ride with Maria Watson, and after that to Mrs Fays where we drank tea and spent the evening—they are very urgent to have us go to the play with them this evening, but I hardly think we shall go—tuesday we stayed at home all the morning—and in the afternon went to drawing school —and from thence to the Battery where we drank tea and spent the evening and this morning I have been reading in the Bible in my Geography—helping Lady Stirling about breakfast waiting upon one of the young ladys who is very sick and have at length seated myself to write to My Dear Papa—Harriet has been very much engaged with her music master—Lady Kitty is this minute eating her

1. Isaac Bronson (also spelled Brunson), banker, was born in Middlebury, Conn. in 1760, served as a junior surgeon during the Revolution, and then traveled to India, China, and Europe. After a try at banking in Hartford and Philadelphia, he settled in New York around 1794. [32 Cortlandt St.] He returned to Connecticut in 1806 and the following year established a bank at Bridgeport. He died in 1838.

breakfast, (she is quite sick) the children have been to school this long time, John has gone to the Office, and William has not yet made his *appearance* and I suppose very probably *will* not these three hours—tho' it is now I believe nearly eleven oclock, but he is frequently in bed till two—and now you have all the things just as they are while I sit upon a little *cricket* with a great book with my paper upon it in my lap, and my ink stand in a chair beside me writing to you—after I have done I intend to wash a little spot of dirt out of my best frock, which I wore to the concert, and which with ironing and smarting up I intend to make do to go to Mr Varicks on friday. We are then going to dress, and Mr Brunson is going to send the carriage at two. And now I am sure Papa I have been particular enough—One thing I must not forget, the other day at Church—Miss Brown had the *kindness* to take me into the *middle* of the isle—and there introduce me to the *Minister* who was wonderfully polite—and promised to call & pay his *respects* to me, she hardly mentioned Harriet, only said "that was my Sister"—I am the favourite with her, I dont know for what reason, unless it is that I look so much like you. She really seems a very clever good hearted woman—and besides seems to have a good deal of *religion*, which is such a rare thing here, that [*it*] quite makes me love her—Harriet says her music master tells her that she must persuade you to get her a new instrument for she improves so fast that she really deserves one. ——————John wishes me to write you that there is to be a paper published here by the former editor of the Walpole paper—which bids fair to be a very fine thing. I suppose he wishes you to subscribe for it[2]—adieu dearest Papa give my very best love to Mama—I shall soon write to her—likewise to Aunt Nabby Hyde and all our dear friends. Your very affectionate & greatfull

MARIA TRUMBULL

2. *The Portfolio* edited by Oliver Oldschool [Joseph Dennie] began publication in mid-January in Philadelphia, not New York (see p. 121).

*To Mrs. Trumbull at Lebanon*

New York [*Saturday*] 17th of January 1800 [*1801*]

My Dear Mama

I am very much obliged to you for your nice long letter. On wednesday after writeing to Papa we dress'd us, and went to Mr Brunsons—there was only several gentlemen to dine. We sat down about half past four and had a very good dinner—we did not spend all the evening—and it was quite lucky that we did not, for about an hour after we came away Mrs Brunson had a fine son born—thursday we did not go out, as it was a rainy day, and were very sorry to miss of our drawing school—we played commerce[1] in the evening and set up till I believe after twelve oclock—the next morning we rose early, eat our breakfast and dressed us to go to Mr Watsons, where we spent as common a very charming day—tho' we got a little cheated, for we expected to have gone in the carriage from there to Mr Varicks—and had upon that account refused going with Mr Benson,[2] who very kindly called in the morning and offered to take us in his carriage—about six oclock we set out for our long expected and *very important* visit—, although it was long after candle light when we got there—yet we were the first—for the rest of the company did not come in an hour, and many in an hour and a half afterwards—we had tea and coffee—and most excellent cake, the ladys were to be sure dressed most *splendidly*—more so than I have ever seen—when tea was over the card tables were set out, and will you believe it

1. A card game played with chips.

2. Robert Benson (1739–1823), lawyer and clerk of the city and county of New York, shortly dismissed from office by the new Republican regime. [8 Pine St.]

dear Mama your poor little Maria was engaged for the first time in her life in playing—for *money*!— — — — I had no idea when I set down to the table that we were *going* to play for money—but Mrs Varick kept asking us, and I was affraid it would look ill natured to refuse—and when we got seated and I saw them all takeing out their money I was to be sure quite in tribulation, for I had not a *single farthing in my pocket*, and every one in the room were entire strangers to me—Harriet was at the other end of the room lookeing over a lieu table[3]—and what to do I knew not. I had never seen a single one of the company till that minute, and they to be sure did not know me *from Adam*—I found my self therefore against my will and *half against* my *conscience* engaged in a game that I had never before seen, and not under *very agreeable circumstances*. Add to all this—I was not only *much* the *youngest* but the most *inexperienced* person in the room, O I am sure had they known my feelings—for a *minute*, they would have *pitied* me from the *bottom* of their *hearts*. However a gentleman who Mrs Varick introduced me to just as we set down, and who was polite enough to offer to instruct me in the game—very kindly and really in a very *friendly* manner, just saying that perhaps it was not convenient for me to put in—*payed for us both*! I felt indeed very much obliged to him—I think he must have seen my confusion, and I suppose pittied the *poor little ignorant girl*. For the first two hands I was extremely lucky, so much so that my instructor expressed much sorrow for he said that good luck in cards denoted much worse success in matters of *far greater importance* and the next deal I was not

3. An oval table designed for the old game of loo.

*sorry* to see a *poor hand enough*—I hardly know whither we *lost* or *won*. I think the *former* however—we played untill I believe eleven or past—when we went in to supper—and never in my life Mama did I see or hardly could I have concieved of any thing so *superb*—there was a monstrous long table—set out with every thing that was nice—and uncommon—a great many different kinds of meats and as for sweet meats nuts fruits—&c &c there was no end to them—such a profusion of every thing that was *rare* and *costly*—we had never before seen—Joined to all this the briliancy of the company—the numerous lights—and the servants in livery—waiting—was such a novel scene that it kept even Harriet almost upon the *grin*. We set forever almost at the table drinking toasts and hearing songs—I drank wine with as many as five or six gentlemen—as for Harriet she would refuse every time, I really think it is wrong in her, at least it looks very *odd*. Mr Varick is I think a most charming man—he seemed to love us so—and treated us with so much kindness I declare I almost felt as if I was by Papa. Mrs Varick too is a dear little woman—and they both begged of us to come very often to see them, indeed they were almost angry that we had been in town so long and had been there so seldom. All the company went away as soon as supper was over (which was I believe about one oclock) except our party—*my good friend and instructor*—and *one* other gentleman. The former was extremely polite, and was for attending us home alone in the carriage, but Mr Varick seemed unwilling, so we waited untill Mr and Mrs Benson—were ready—he would go in with us then however—and we had a sweet ride home. Mrs Benson is a very fine woman—and her husband, is a *polished*

*Walter Woodworth*,[4] they seemed very friendly indeed to us—the folks were all very glad to see us at home—and upon the whole we spent a very pleasant day—I found that the gentleman who was so kind to me, was a young gentleman, who had been much abroad had resided a short time in England, dissipated a large fortune and is now doing I know not what, he was acquainted with Uncle John, and as he is a very clever good hearted man, I felt quite glad that I had so *good* an instructor. Thus ended this important day. This morning we have been out makeing calls—in the afternoon to drawing school, and drank tea with Lady Kitty at Mrs *Phil Livingstons*.[5] And now dear Mama you have our weeks adventures and as it grows late, and I have a good deal to do and besides have not been to bed very early these two or three nights—and farther as this letter is not a very short one, I will with Harriets and my best love to dear Papa and all friends subscribe myself your very greatfull and affectionate daughter

MARIA TRUMBULL

4. (1731–1805). Lived in Lebanon.

5. In 1790, at the age of 50, Lady Kitty's courtly cousin, "Gentleman Phil," had taken a young wife and now had a house full of little children. [40 Broadway.]

*To Mrs. Trumbull at Lebanon*

New York [*Monday*] January 18th 1801

Dear Mama

I have to acknowledge the receipt of a letter from you by Mr Morgan. I wrote to you the same day that he arrived in town, and hope the letter has reached you long before this. Maria received a letter from you on thursday, by which we are informed that you have returned to Lebanon, I trust that you found every thing as it should be and in good order, that Aunt Nabby had made a great deal of nice butter, does Sylvia remain with you yet? and who does Papa expect to have in Simons place,[1] I am very glad you have got a little girl, as I think attending to and teaching her will be a great amusement to you, I hope she will prove very good, and of great use to you, both now and when she grows older, I long to see her and teach her to read and work. I wish to hear very much how you find yourself my dear Mama since your return, but suppose we shall have no letters again till Thursday. I hope the giddiness you complain of, will soon be removed, and that you will enjoy yourself very well this winter, and not feel any anxiety on our account, as we do very well indeed; one quarter of the time allotted for our absence is elapsed, and does not seem like any thing at all, the remainder of the time will soon be gone, and we shall be rejoiced to return home to see our dear friends; we have already and doubtless shall make more acquaintances that we shall part with, with regret, Maria Watson in particular is a dear good girl,

1. Sylvia, Simon, Edmund (p. 88), Tom, Betsy, and John McCurdy (p. 122) were farm and domestic helpers of various ages. According to family letters, the male turnover was frequent, but Betsy remained with the Trumbulls until 1806 and Sylvia was still with them in 1810.

and treats us with very great kindness and affection, she thinks of making a long visit at Hartford next summer and I hope we shall be able to persuade her to go to Lebanon; we go to Mr Watsons frequently, but are always impatient to have Fridays come when we go very early and pass such a pleasant day, that we almost hate to come away, at Mr Sebors too they are very good to us.

Last Monday we drank tea at Mrs Fays. Mary Austin has been staying there for a few days past. Nancy Austin, a Miss Kinsey, and Mrs Bradley, Mr Phelps, Mr Cumming and Mr Gautier, were there, we spent the evening there and were entertained by the ladies singing, tuesday we went to drawing school and went to Mr Watsons without an invitation, to drink tea, we found Roswell Colt here when we returned, Wednesday we went to Mr Brunsons to dine, we met Weltha Morgan, her Papa two Mr Phelp's and two other gentlemen there, we did not sit down to table till after four, the latest we have ever dined except at Mr Churches, we had candles before we had done, we had a very excellent dinner and every thing in an elegant style, we drank tea there and about an hour after we came away, Mrs Brunson had a fine son, Thursday it rain'd and we staid at home all day, and could not go to drawing school, Friday we went to Mr Watsons and dined, in the afternoon Mr McCracken[2] came in, he had before call'd at our house and left letters for us, but we were obliged to restrain our impatience to read them till our return from the Mayors where we were to pass the evening, we went from Mr

2. John McCracken (1775–1833), Hartford merchant, married Rebecca Hopkins (p. 151, n. 2) in June. He moved to New York about 1811–1812.

Watsons about six OClock, Mr H Hudson walked there with us, none of the company came till we had been there half an hour, when we had tea and coffee, and excellent plumb and pound cake. After that the company play'd cards all but one young lady and myself and between ten and eleven we sat down to the most elegant supper I could conceive of, the table was elegantly set with a great deal of glass and a large pyramid in the centre, there was a boiled turkey, roast ducks, partridges, a variety of birds, fryed oysters, tongues, and other things that I did not know, a great quantity of pies puddings and nick nack, with jellies, syllabubs, sweetmeats, &c, and oranges, apples, nuts, almonds, grapes and raisins. Mr & Mrs Ray, Mr and Mrs Gracie, Mr and Mrs Benson, Miss Rogers Miss Lambert, two Mr Lawrences, Mr Lambert Miss Bleeker and Mr Kissam, were the company,[3] we came away after twelve with Mrs Benson who was so good as to bring us home in her carriage, and was very polite in asking us to her house; Mr and Mrs Varick were also very polite and attentive to us indeed, and we both almost fell in love with him, he inquired after Papa. Saturday we walked out in the morning, went to drawing school, and drank tea with Lady Kitty and the young ladies at Mr Livingstons, yesterday we went to church, dined with Mrs Sebor and went to church with her in the afternoon, Miss Eliza Atkinson drank tea there, to day we go with Lady Kitty and some other members of the family to dine at Lady Mary Watts's, and Wednesday

3. Cornelius Ray and Archibald Gracie, merchants. Miss Rogers, Miss Lambert, and Mr. Lambert were nieces and nephew of Mrs. Gracie (Esther Rogers) who was the sister of Henry, Nehemiah, and Moses Rogers (p. 119, n. 3) and of Mrs. David Lambert (Susannah Rogers).

we are engaged to meet Miss Howland Miss Atkinson and some young Ladys at Mr Sebors, so the time passes my dear Mama in visiting and gadding about, I do long sometimes to stay quietly at home for a few days; our drawing I fear will come on but poorly as we are obliged to lose so many days, and my music master disappoints me too frequently, he says however that I do very well and must try to persuade my Papa to get me a good instrument, as I deserve a better than the one I hire of him which is a miserable thing, but I dont think it will be best to have one while I stay here. Mrs Sebor wishes us to go to dancing school with her daughter who is to begin soon, we wish you and Papa to determine whether it is best; it would be well perhaps for us to go one quarter, but still it seems quite unnecessary as we have not danced any, and see no prospect of it while we stay, and it will be an additional expense, we have received from Colonel or General Giles[4] tickets for the assembly to attend during the season, but have no idea of going. We have got us some white gowns, and employed a woman recommended by Mrs Sebor to make them, she charged us a pritty good price, but all mantua makers do who take in work here, I suppose we might have a woman come to the house who would work much cheaper, if it was right to occasion so much trouble to Lady Kitty, we have not got the calico for Maria yet as I thought it was best to wait a little longer for that from home but I think

4. Aquila Giles was one of the founders of the Columbian Anacreontic Society and often had a guiding hand in the assemblies and various other affairs at which New York socialites amused themselves. He was dismissed from his office as United States Marshal for the District of New York shortly after the election of President Jefferson.

she has no immediate necessity for it; We have thought some of getting us some persians, they are beginning to be much worn here, and are to be had a good deal cheaper than we have ever had, at only nine and sixpence, this money, they would be very convenient on many occasions, if mine was darker I should not think of it, and as it is if you dont think it quite best they are by no means necessary. I believe [*torn*] Huntington[5] has not wrote to Lady Kitty about taking Harriet as I heard nothing of it and I think I should if he had. You need not fear Mama that we shall be troubled with civilities from the Churches, the young ladies have never call'd to see us, they have parties every week to which young ladies of our age and acquaintance are invited, but we have never received invitations, to our great joy. Mr & Mrs Little call'd to see us one day this week but we were out. We see Uncle Backus often, he inquires when we hear from home, and desires his love. This is a long letter my dear Mama, and it is time I was dressing to go out. With my very best love to dear Papa, and to all Lebanon friends I remain your ever gratefull and very affectionate daughter

HARRIET TRUMBULL

5. General Jedediah Huntington of New London, Conn., who came to New York on business in May (p. 171), perhaps contemplated bringing his 17-year-old daughter Harriet to live with Lady Kitty.

*To Mrs. Trumbull at Lebanon*

New York [*Monday*] 26th January 1800 [*1801*]

DEAR MAMA

Mr Lanman call'd this evening while we were out, to tell us that he was going to Connecticut, and if we wish'd to write we must send our letters to him tomorrow, so that I have but a few moments to write, to thank you for your good letter which I received on Thursday, I am extremely obliged to you dear Mama, for writing me so much when you are so troubled with a giddiness in your head, but I hope that complaint has already, or will very soon leave you, that you may write with more ease to yourself. I wrote a long letter to you last week, which I suppose will reach you tomorrow, in the stage; I sent it to sister by Mr Morgan, by whom we wrote ten long letters, and four more, [*by*] Mr McCracken, we were a good while writing them to besure, as we do not have much time to devote to writing to any but our own family. I am sorry that I did not know of Mr Lanmans intention of visiting Norwich, sooner, as I could then have procured your brushes and put them under his care, tho he may be going in the stage and it would not be convenient for him, I shall probably have an opportunity again soon; I fancy some of our Cousins will be not a little glad to see the above named gentleman, perhaps Lebanon may be enlivened by a wedding.[1] I saw Joseph Howland[2] (who is [*in*] town) on Saturday, he rather appear'd to think that John Trumbull[3] would not return

1. Peter Lanman married Cousin Abby Trumbull in December 1801.

2. Betsy Howland's brother, who had just graduated from Yale in September.

3. Uncle David Trumbull's 16-year-old son John went to sea instead of returning to college and in May wrote from England of seeing Uncle John Trumbull and his bride.

to Colledge again, what a pity that he should have taken such a dislike to study. I left my journal at last Monday evening, Tuesday it stormed in the morning and was such bad walking that we did not go out at all, even to drawing school but busied ourselves in writing letters, in the evening Mr McCracken, and Roswell Colt and Henry Hudson call'd to see us, Wednesday morning we call'd to see Mrs Benson, and Mrs Little, who were both very polite to us, we dined at Mr Sebors, and in the afternoon went with Mrs Sebor to dancing school, she wished to see if she liked the school as she talks of sending her daughter, we were very much pleased with it,[4] Mrs and two Miss Atkinsons, and Miss Storer[5] dranke tea there, and in the evening some gentlemen came in, and we played and frolicked all the evening, and had a little supper of biscuits and sweetmeats, nuts and apples, thursday we went to drawing school, and to tea at Mr Watsons where we spent the evening and had the honour of seeing Colonel Pickering.[6] Friday we went to Mr Watsons again, and passed a very pleasant day, and as usual had Roswell Colt to attend us home, he is the very best young man I know; Saturday it was an unpleasant day, and snowed some but we went to

4. The school of M. Lalliet, who held his classes at Mr. Little's Hotel on Broad St. (see also p. 155, n. 2) *Daily Advertiser*, March 31.

5. Eliza and Mary Ann, daughters of John Atkinson, merchant. [20 Cortlandt St.] Miss Storer was their cousin.

6. Timothy Pickering, United States Secretary of State from 1795 until May 1800 when John Adams dismissed him for obstructing presidential policies. Pickering, guided by Alexander Hamilton, opposed Adams' proposal for sending a peace mission to France to negotiate differences that had brought the United States to the verge of war.

drawing school, in spite of weather and walking. Sunday we went to church, all day, dined at Mr Sebors, and had that gentleman to walk home with us in the evening. This morning the Miss Murrays[7] call'd to see us, they were very friendly indeed, said they should have been to see us sooner, but did not know we were in town till Mr James Wadsworth[8] told them, their Papa was almost angry with ours because he did not write by us to let him know we were here; they invited us to dine with them on Wednesday in a friendly way, to come early and at all times without ceremony; this afternoon we drank tea with Lady Kitty and the young ladies and gentlemen at Mrs Peter Livingstons. I suppose by this time my dear Mama Papa has received a letter from me, enclosing a little account of my expenses only,[9] tho he had not desired me to do it I thought it was time to let him know how fast money ran away; next month I intend sending another; when Brother paid Lady Kitty some money while he was in town, she said she should not

7. Mary and Hannah, daughters of the merchant-philanthropist John Murray, were about ten years older than Harriet and Maria. [269 Pearl St.]

8. A 32-year-old bachelor from Connecticut who was engaged in promoting the settlement of New York State along the Genesee River, where he owned land and managed the huge tracts owned by Jeremiah Wadsworth (sister Faith's father-in-law). He was also at this time acting as guardian for the illegitimate son of Uncle John Trumbull, a responsibility that was a little later transferred to the Murrays.

9. The following addition occurs on the outside of this letter: $32 plus $43.55 equals $75.55 (the girls' expenditures); £13.10.8 plus £3.17.3 equals £17.7.11 (probably the amounts received by the girls from Mr. Sebor. See p. 88). In spite of the adoption of a national coinage in 1792, Americans in 1801 still reckoned in pounds, shillings, and pence as well as in dollars and cents.

wish to receive any more until the first of February, which is close by, when I will remember it. Maria desires her best love, please to give mine also to dear Papa, to all Lebanon friends by no means forgetting Aunt Nabby, and believe me dear Mama, your very dutiful and affectionate daughter

HARRIET TRUMBULL

New York [*Monday*] 26th of January 1801

My Dear Papa

I have left the Journal for this week to Harriet and am going to give you an account of my expences —since I have been here—it is just two months to day, and I declare it almost frightens me to think how fast the *time* and the *money* have run away—and yet upon looking over the accounts I dont think I have been extravagant but money does go strangely. However I hardly think we shall spend as *much* for the future, as there were a good many things to be got that wont be again—the whole that I have spent amounts to 43 dollars, 4 shillings, and 7 pence,[1] and that you may know what has become of it I have sent an exact *list* of every thing—the most unnecessary thing is the 2 and sixpence of sugar plumbs—but there are so many little sweet good things, that I cant resist the temptation of tasteing them once and a while—about the *trinket* which you will se set down—I must clear *myself*—as I should be sorry to have my Dear Papa think that I would spend his money for such foolish things—for *myself* at least—but the long and the short of the matter is this—Sally Colt[2] has several times made us little presents—and within a week or two—she has sent us some very handsome *Nelson balls*[3] (*Sally Trumbull can tell you what they are*) and we thought we could do no less than send her some little fashionable

1. Endorsement on reverse of letter: "with a/c $43.55."
2. Nineteen-year-old sister of Roswell Colt.
3. Nelson balls were small gilt buttons used in ornamental rows on clothing and on bed and window cornices. Many items were named in honor of Admiral Horatio Nelson after his victory over the French in the battle of the Nile, 1798. For this reference I am indebted to Mrs. Anne W. Murray and Miss Rodris Roth, both of the Smithsonian Institution.

trinket in return—we of course got one, as pretty as we could—it cost a dollar and a quarter—and is the only thing of the kind that we have even *asked* the *price* of since we have been here. The *hair dressing* business to be sure was nonsense, and I have heartily repented it ever since—but Lady Kitty thought it would not be proper to go to the Concert with my hair plain as I generally wear it, and hair dressers you know Papa wont work for nothing so there went one dollar for no other purpose than makeing me look as *much* like a witch as such a *pretty girl as I can look*—and now dear Papa I hope you will think I have been quite *prudent* considering what an *extravagant* girl I am. I dont believe *Weltha Morgans* account would show to much better advantage—her Papa when he was in town got her a pair of pearl earrings that cost 28 dollars!—and I must confess I think it was a very foolish piece of extravagance.[4] I would not thank *my Papa* for such a present.

I really think this is quite a letter of business so far—and now I am going to send my very best love to all Uncle Trumbulls family—Aunt Williams, cousins Solomon and William[5]—Miss Anna—and Mary—Aunt Nabby Dutton—Miss Lydia Robinson, Mrs Hyde and her daughters[6]—Mrs

4. John Morgan was not a man to hide his wealth. In 1785, in the first American ship ever to enter Chinese waters, he imported a large quantity of made-to-order chinaware bearing his name and coat of arms. He was, said his nephew, "aristocratic in feeling and bearing," one of a group of princely Hartford merchants who affected the proud dignity of lords and nobles to the manor born.

5. Sons of Aunt Williams. William later married cousin Sally Trumbull.

6. Widow of Ebenezer Hyde who was captured by the British during the Revolution and died on the crowded Jersey prison ship. Her daughters were Eunice and Elizabeth, aged 21 and 22.

Tisdale—Aunt Betty[7]—Aunt Sarah Doctor Thad—and particularly to Aunt Nabby Hyde who I hope is still in the practice of makeing good pies and cake— —and pray dont forget Sally.—I do want so to fly to Lebanon sometimes that I dont know what to do. Mama must contrive to keep of [*off*] the heighpo as much as possible—I am sure writing to us will do her good and we will promise her good long letters in return—adieu dearest Papa accept the best love of your Dutifull & affectionate child

MARIA TRUMBULL

7. Probably Betty Southworth of whom Harriet wrote in 1806:

> I have one piece of information which you will be sorry to hear, at a meeting for the selling the poor this week, Mr Gillet bought Aunt Betty Southworth, the poor old lady is very much distressed at the idea of being taken away from all her friends and acquaintance, I went to see her yesterday, she cried, and said she never expected to see me again, and that I must give her love to you and to Mr Hudson and tell you that she was very thankful for all your kindnesses: Mr Gillet has talk'd some of coming into this neighborhood, and I hope that she will not be carried away.

April 2, to Faith Wadsworth, Silliman Family Collection. Small towns that could not support an almshouse sold the services of the indigent and elderly to the highest bidder who would house and feed them. The proceeds went to pay for the maintenance (also in private families) of those who could no longer work.

*To Mrs. Trumbull at Lebanon*

New York [*Wednesday*] 4th of February 1801

My Dear Mama

It is a great while since you have heared what we are about here, and I will now begin with last tuesday—in the morning we set out to make some calls but found the walking so bad—and Harriet had so bad a cold, that she turned back, I however went to the Battery—where they kept me to dinner—and I went from thence to drawing school—in the evening we wrote, read and played cards—till twelve oclock—we really have got into a bad habit of sitting up very late, we seldom get to bed before twelve—and many of the family sit up much later—wednesday we were to have gone to Mr Murrays—but the badness of the weather and walking prevented us—thursday it rained very much—however we made out to get to drawing school tho' to besure the walking was *bad enough*—we had company to tea and spend the evening—friday morning Mr Brunson called to ask us to tea—and to go to the play in the evening—but as we were engaged to Mr Watsons we refused—to go—even to the play—dont you think Mama that we have been quite moderate—to go to only one play in eight weeks tho we have had so many invitations? we spent a charming day and evening at Mr Watsons—and were attended home as usual by Mr Colt and Mr Hudson—saturday morning—we were at home drawing all the morning—Miss Morgan and Miss Ivers called to se us—in the afternoon we went to drawing school—sunday we were at Church all day—and had an excellent sermone—the *fun* of it is that by going to two different Churches we get the same sermon all day[1] but however as it is generally a good one I believe it wont hurt us—we dined and drank tea as usual at Mr Sebors—we found Uncle Backus when we got home—he is the *querest* man that ever I saw—he knows every body and every thing—and yet no body seems to know him—Monday morning Mr Eben Watson[2] and Harry Hudson called from Mrs Watson to ask us to drink tea with her and go to the play in the evening—and I can assure you we accepted the invitation with pleasure—after they were gone we set out upon an expedition to call all about town, and a long walk to besure we had—we went to Mrs Brunsons General Stevens's,[3] Miss Murrays, Mr Glovers—Mrs Varricks Mrs Sebors—Mrs Coits, Mrs Atkinsons, and Mrs Stuarts returned got

1. The pastors of St. Paul's and Trinity apparently followed the common practice of exchanging pulpits for the afternoon service, and repeating their morning sermon to the different audience.

2. Ebenezer Watson (1776–1847), formerly of Hartford, nephew and business partner of James Watson. In August 1801 the partnership was dissolved and Eben went into business with his half-brother Henry Hudson (p. 81). Eben's widowed mother had married Barzillai Hudson in 1779 and Henry was born in 1780. Henry's father succeeded Eben's father as publisher (with George Goodwin) of Hartford's *Connecticut Courant*, and Henry was later taken into the business.

3. Ebenezer Stevens (1751–1832). [59 Beekman St.] Harriet and Maria were calling on his 20-year-old daughter, Rebecca. See Harriet's list of calls made on this day (p. 113). Stevens, born in Boston and married to a Hartford girl, had entered business in New York right after the Revolution and had become one of the city's most successful merchants in foreign trade. Like most of the older men in these letters he had also pursued a public and military career, which for him began with participating in the Boston Tea Party. Most recently, as a result of the French war scare, he had been placed in charge of fortifying New York harbor and had been given the rank of full brigadier general.

our dinner about half past three, and then went to the Battery—and from thence to the play where we were tolerably entertained with the Force of Calumny, and Tom Thumb[4]—we had Mr Watson Mr Hudson Mr Colt and

4. The girls also saw M. Laurence perform "the peasant's dance." *The Force of Calumny* was a five act play translated from *Die Verlaumder* of August von Kotzebue, a German dramatist several of whose works were in vogue at the Park Theater this winter. The final piece on the program was billed as "a musical Burletta, called The Tragedy of Tragedies, with the life and Death of TOM THUMB THE GREAT." Benjamin Silliman (Harriet's future husband) saw this play in London in 1805 and described it as follows:

> The after-piece was *Tom Thumb*, of giant killing memory. The little story which we used to read in our three-penny picture books, detailing the adventures of this pigmy hero, is much more interesting than the stupid farrago which they have wrought into the dramatic form. I will not tire and disgust you by an account of the strange crudities, and monstrous doings of every kind, which followed each other, tonight, in rapid and ominous succession. The catastrophe was certainly the most gratifying incident, as it was the last, and indeed it had quite as much of nature in it as any portion of the performance.
>
> The doughty hero, Tommy Thumb, a little boy, in scarlet, about 40 inches high, after wonderful deeds of valour, in single combat, by which he wins a beautiful princess—that is to say, a coarse athletic actress, tall enough for a grenadier—is just on the point of making her his bride, when, terrible to relate, a great English cow, steps from behind the scenes, and, at one mighty gulp, swallows Tommy down, sword and all. The thing was received with great applause, and indeed almost every thing succeeds when trick'd off with the decorations of the stage.
>
> In the performances this evening, there was much gross indecency of language without any natural connection with the plot, and thrown in merely to catch the populace. It is really farcical to talk of the morality of the stage, unless there are theaters differently conducted from any that I have yet seen either in this country or my own.

*A Journal of Travels . . . 1805 and 1806* (N.Y. 1810) I, 325.

Mr Fisk[5] for beaux.—Lady Kitty went out to tea and it stormed so much that she stayed all night—and left the young folks to keep house—the next morning—we eat breakfast and spent the forenoon by ourselves—Lady Kitty did not return till dinner time—we went to drawing school in the afternoon and drank tea and spent the evening at Mr Murrays—they are charming people and treat us very kindly and affectionately—the young ladies are very accomplished indeed—and Mr and Mrs Murray—are plain good *quakers,*[6] they live in a very large house in Pearl Street —and are very rich—Mr Murray seems to have been well acquainted with Papa—we enjoyed ourselves extremely and did not return till quite late in the evening. This morning Harriet has been takeing her lesson in music and is practiceing—her master is very attentive of late—we are going by and by to call at Mrs Churches and from there to Mrs Coits to dine—and now my dear Mama you have the particulars—we are very happy here—and I beg of you not to trouble yourself about us even if we should some times write a little low spirited. Lady Kitty is really a lovely good woman—and the only thing that troubles me is the young mens swearing so much, the eldest at least—for John has almost entirely left it off since we have been here— and you will now hardly hear him make use of an oath once

5. John B. Fisk, tutor of young James Watson. See Harriet to Eliza Sebor Jan. 15, 1806, Silliman Family Collection and *The Spectator* Jan. 8, 1806.

6. Mrs. Murray (Hannah Lindley of Philadelphia) was a Quaker, but had been disowned by the Philadelphia Monthly Meeting when she married John Murray (1737–1808) who was not a Quaker. The family thereafter attended the First Presbyterian Church in New York and had their children baptized there.

a week, tho he *used not to be very spareing* of them. The young ladies are pretty girls—enough—I wish Papa would write us what we had best to do about offering Mr Watson money for our play tickets—I spoke to Maria and asked her to say something to her Uncle about it, but she said "No indeed that we must not be so scrupulous"—Harriet desires her best love to all friends—Papa in particular—pray remember me very affectionately to him—and my best love to *all* my Lebanon friends—adieu my dear Mama keep up your spirits—and believe me your very gratefull and dutifull daughter

MARIA TRUMBULL

*To Mrs. Trumbull at Lebanon*

New York [*Wednesday*] 11th of February 1800 [*1801*]

Dear Mama

It is really a long time since I have written to you, and I know not what excuse to make but only that as Maria has more time than I have, I am willing she should do the most writing, we had the pleasure of receiving a company letter from you last Thursday, and we are much obliged to you for it, tho we feel grateful for your goodness in writing once a week yet I cant help wishing sometimes that we could hear oftener, I should like to have a letter one day from Lebanon, and the next from Hartford all the time we stay: we expect to hear tomorrow, and I hope Mr Lanman will return soon, as we shall expect a letter by him. As it is so long since I have written I must carry my journal as far back as I can remember which is two Sundays ago, we went to church and spent the day with our dear good Mrs Sebor, Monday morning we call'd at Mrs Brunsons, at Miss Stevens's, at the Miss Murrays, at Mr Glovers[1] to see Weltha, at Colonel Varicks, and at Mrs Sebors to get her to make more calls with us, we went then to Mrs Coits, Mrs Atkinsons, and Mrs Stewarts,[2] we then came home and dined and went to Mr Watsons to tea and to the play in the evening, I wish Papa to tell me what

1. Weltha Morgan was apparently staying at the home of the merchant John I. Glover who had come from Leeds, England, before the Revolution. [223 Pearl St.] Though his main commercial interests were in New York he also had had a firm in New Haven for several years.

2. The former Jane Winthrop, sister of Mrs. Jacob Sebor, Mrs. Adolphus Yates and Mr. Francis Bayard Winthrop. Her husband, William Stewart, died in 1798, a few years after they moved from New London to New York. She was probably now living with one of her Stewart relatives on Greenwich St., a near neighbor, perhaps, of the Barclay girls in whose company she is always mentioned.

I must do when we go to the play about paying for our tickets, I dont like to take them for nothing, and I am so foolish I dont know how to offer money. Tuesday we went to drawing school and drank tea with the Miss Murrays, they are the finest women I have seen here, very amiable and accomplished, they draw elegantly, one of them has taken the likenesses of all the family, they have an excellent instrument and play and sing delightfully, they treat us in a very friendly manner and like Connecticut people, Wednesday we dined at Mrs Coits with Betsey Howland, and as it was a stormy evening we had a carriage to come home in, Thursday the walking was too bad for us to go to school, Friday we went to Mr Watsons, Miss Taylor dined there, and Miss Howland Miss Morgan, Mr Glover,[3] and Mr Phillips[4] drank tea and passed the evening there, I staid all night and slept with Maria Watson, our Maria came home, Saturday we both went to drawing school. Sunday morning we went to the Roman Catholic Chapel[5] with Miss Morgan Miss Howland and Mr Phillips, we dined at Mrs Sebors and went to church with her, Betsey Howland and Mr Phillips drank tea with us there, Monday we went to Mrs Sebors and dined on cold beef with Eliza,[6] and went to dancing school, yesterday Maria went to Mr Watsons

3. Probably young Thomas Glover (son of Daniel) from Leeds, England who married Weltha Morgan in December.

4. George Thompson Phillips (b. 1782, son of "General" George Phillips of Middletown, Conn.) was probably at this time working for Levi Coit (p. 59, n. 5) who later took him into partnership and sent him to New Orleans to manage the company business there.

5. St. Peter's in Barclay St., built in 1784. Visiting St. Peter's, like visiting the Battery and the Park Theater, was one of the things that tourists did in New York, especially if they came from parts of the country where Roman Catholics were a rarity.

6. The Sebors' eldest child. (1787–1855).

and spent the day and went to drawing school, I did not [*go*] for I have an eruption on my skin which I rather think is the Chicken Pox, Lady Kitty insisted tho I was quite well that I should not go out for fear I might take cold. It was very cold last night and is so to day, it has been snowing all day and I dare say it will be good sleighing with you, and Sister and Brother will go to Lebanon. I wish some of our friends would come to New York, there were three houses burnt last night and two children and a black woman in them,[7] it was a dreadful night for it stormed and the wind was very high.

7. The *Commercial Advertiser* (Feb. 11) reported that no lives were lost and that the two recently imported pumping engines had conveyed water by suction from the river (460 feet away) in such quantity that "the ranks now became of no use, greatly to the satisfaction of some hundreds of citizens, who were handing the water." On March 4, however, the *Daily Advertiser* carried a notice from the fire wardens stating that

> it is well known by those that were eye-witnesses that most of the water that was the happy mean of arresting the progress of the fire alluded to, was handed in buckets by the inhabitants from the wells and cisterns in Gold, Cliff and John streets. It is therefore the earnest request of the Fire Wardens, to their fellow citizens, not to be lull'd into a state of security by the publication alluded to, so as to be prevented from supplying themselves with the requisite number of buckets, but wish when the cry of fire is heard, they would bring their buckets with them; and immediately form themselves into ranks with alacrity as our safety under providence depends on a speedy and full supply of water.

The buckets were used to fill engines which, by hand pumping (several men on each side), provided a stream of water that could be directed at the flames. Buckets bore their owners' names and, after a fire was extinguished, were piled in a designated location from which they were to be promptly retrieved so as to be ready for the next fire. The long hoses of the new fire engines (also hand-operated) could deliver river water to the pumping engines at the fire site or spray the fire directly if its distance and height from the river did not cause too great a reduction in water pressure.

We have not been out to get our persian yet but intend it as soon as the weather will permit and Mrs Sebor can go with us, we have never worn our new white gowns but are keeping [*them*] for a party at Mr Murrays in a fortnight, to which we are invited. I hardly know what to say about the cheese you thought of sending to Lady Kitty my dear Mama, they are all fond of it, but I dont know how they would like a *present*; we live very well, and no one would ever guess at her poverty by seeing our dinner tables. I am sorry you think of having us return so soon, not but what I would be glad to go, even next week, but I wish to make out two quarters in music and drawing, music especially I dislike to leave as it is probably the only time I shall ever have for learning it, Mr. Hewitt[8] comes very regularly, and says he is well satisfied with my improvement, yet I can make *but* little progress in six months, and *less time* would only be throwing money away; I hope therefore dear Mama that you and Papa will consent to let us stay longer, and not think we dont wish to see you for I assure you we do more than any thing. I have sent Papa my account again. I hope he will find it reasonable but washing is a great expense to us, tho we endeavour to be as fr[ugal?] as possible, and appear decent, we wear white very little, but I fear our bills will be increased by going to dancing school. However the persians will be very usefull. Papa will see by the money we have received from Mr Sebor how much he has remaining, I am most frightend sometimes

8. James Hewitt (1770–1827) was not only a teacher of music but a prolific composer of vocal and instrumental pieces, operettas, and incidental theater music. He was also conductor and musician at concerts and at the Park Theater, and he ran a music store in Maiden Lane.

with all our economy, but we must try to be very prudent, that I may not lose my piano forte. This is very bad writing my dear Mama but I hope you can read it, my best love to dear Papa, and my kind regards to all other friends as also Marias, hoping to hear tomorrow that you are better I remain dear Mama your grateful and affectionate daughter

Harriet

how does your little girl come on

*To Mrs. Trumbull at Lebanon*

New York [*Wednesday*] 18th February 1801

Dear Mama

We were very happy last thursday to receive letters from you by Mr Lanman, and to see a person who had just come from Lebanon, and probably seen you and our dear Papa, I wish to see you both, more than I can express, and am always rejoiced to receive letters, Mr Lanman told us that Brother and Sister were going to Lebanon, the day after he was in Hartford, and we have since received letters from Sister informing that she was going to make you a visit; and Maria yesterday received a letter from her written at Lebanon by which we are very glad to hear that she found you dear Mama, better in health and spirits than she expected, we hope to hear the same account from yourself tomorrow, I am glad Sister intends making you so long a visit, how I should like to be at home with you, I hope she will be able to persuade you to return with her to spend the month of March at Hartford for I am sure it will be much pleasanter for you, and for her too, and as I think it will [*be*] some inducement, consider how much oftener you will hear from us; for we will write three or four times a week. As I know you will like to know what we have been doing lately, I will continue my journal from the time I wrote you last Mama, which was Wednesday; it snowed so hard all that day that we were confined to the house and could not go to dancing school, we employed and amused ourselves as well as we could, and played cards in the evening, Thursday it was extremely cold but we wrapped up warm, and went to Mrs Sebors early to dine and go to dancing school with Eliza, we took our lesson and got to drawing school before three OClock, in the evening Mr Lanman call'd and brought us letters, and Maria Watson came to see us, we played cards again and eat supper, and went to bed late, three bad things, Friday morning I took a music lesson, it was terrible cold but I had a fire,[1] we went to Mr Watsons where we found old Judge Hobart[2] who is there a great deal, and Mr Woollcot, in the afternoon it began to snow, but Mrs. Rogers, Mrs Hopkins, and Mrs William Woolsey[3] with their husbands drank tea there, Mrs Woolsey apologized for not having call'd to see us, by saying that she had been very much confined by sickness in her family, but as they were all well now, she should call, she said we ought not to stand upon ceremony with an old married woman; we had some time before met old Mrs Woolsey,[4] at Mr George

1. The temperature was fourteen degrees at 8:00 A.M. Diary of Henry Laight.

2. James Sloss Hobart (1738–1805), judge of the United States District Court for New York, was a native of Fairfield, Conn. and a graduate of Yale, but had lived in New York since before the Revolution.

3. William Walton Woolsey (1766–1839) lived at 334 Pearl St. and was the brother of George Muirson Woolsey. The Woolsey family had moved from Long Island to Fairfield County, Conn. after the death of their father in 1771. When the family fortune was wiped out by the Revolution, the boys were put to work at an early age in New York mercantile houses, and in due time they headed prosperous firms of their own. Their half-sister, Sarah Woolsey, was the Mrs. Rogers at the Watsons' tea party. Her husband, Moses Rogers (1750–1825) had moved from Norwalk, Conn. early in the 1780's and was now one of New York's most successful merchants. [272 Pearl St.] The Rogers' daughter, Sarah, was the Mrs. Hopkins at the party. She had, in October, married Samuel Miles Hopkins (1772–1837) who left Connecticut in 1794. After a few years in business, as an associate of Mr. Watson, Hopkins had turned to the practice of law. [16 Broad St.]

4. Mrs. Benjamin Woolsey, Jr. was the mother of William Walton Woolsey, George Muirson Woolsey, and Mrs. William Dunlap (wife of the manager of the Park Theater); the stepmother of Mrs. Moses

Woolseys, she had made the same excuses for her daughter, and asked us to call, which we intended doing but we have already so many acquaintances, and so many things to do, that we cant find time to *make*, only to *return* calls, except to some particular *married* ladies, to whom such respect is due, for attention to us, it stormed so much on Friday night, that Mr Watson insisted upon keeping us there, and as he would have been obliged to hire a carriage to send us home (for his coachman has conducted so ill lately that he wont permit him to drive) we *gladly consented* to stay, for we are always happy to stay there, we dined there Saturday, and they got a sleigh to send us to drawing school, Maria Watson went with us for the ride, and Henry Hudson who was our beau, persuaded us, that as we were in the sleigh it was as well to go a little farther, so we had a very pleasant ride two or three miles out of town, and got to drawing school in quite good season. The Miss Watts[5] who go to school with us, were coming here at night, *and very politely* offered to take us home in the sleigh with them. Sunday we went to church, and to Mr Sebors, Mr and Mrs Corp call'd to take Mrs Sebor to ride, and invited me to go with them, we rode out of town several miles and returned in time to dine and go to church in the afternoon, we came from there early, and Roswell Colt came here and spent the evening, Monday I took a music lesson in the morning, dined with Eliza Sebor and went to dancing school and to drink tea at Mrs Corps, with Mrs Sebor and

---

Rogers and Mrs. Timothy Dwight (wife of the president of Yale); and daughter of Dr. George Muirson, Jr., the inventor and first practitioner of mercurial inoculation for smallpox.

5. Anne and Catherine, daughters of Lady Mary Watts.

several other Ladies, we returned early and spent the evening at Mrs Sebors and sup'd on bread and sweetmeats, Tuesday Maria and I set out to go to drawing one before the other different ways, it began to rain and I turned back thinking she would also, but she did not, and it rain'd very hard all the afternoon, and she walked home as wet as could be, but she changed her cloathes directly and did not take cold, I sent to get a carriage for her, but she was too quick, there were several ladies at school, and most of them rode, the Miss Watts were there too, and had their sleigh sent for them but did not offer to take her home, which I think was a great shame. We see Miss Morgan at School but dont meet her often elsewhere, we are to drink tea with her tomorrow at Mrs Coits if the weather will permit, she appears to be cheerful and contented, but I dont think she visits much. Papa mentions our subscribing his name to a paper lately began to be published, the young gentlemen here have subscribed, we have seen the numbers that have come out, and agree with them in thinking they are poor things, and that Papa would not be plea[sed with th]em, besides they are published in Philadelphia, not in New Yo[rk. We adm]ired Colonel Pickering, but he was very different in his appearance, from the opinion I had formed of him, I think he resembles Papa a little about his mouth, and I loved him for that; we were charmed with Mr Wollcot,[6] he staid at Mr Watsons, there

6. Oliver Wolcott (1760–1833), ex-Secretary of the United States Treasury. He had a few weeks earlier resigned his post and was now returning to Connecticut. His brother, Frederick, a judge in the Probate District Court of Litchfield, Conn. had recently married the daughter of Col. Joshua Huntington of Norwich.

was a great dinner given to him last Monday at the Coffee House. I think if his Brother is like him, Colonel and Mrs. Huntington are very happy that their daughter has so good an husband; and I hope he is. I enclosed in my last letter, another account, I am rather fearful it will never reach you, and wish to know if it does; if Papa still thinks it best, we will subscribe to that paper, it may possibly sometimes contain something that would amuse him; We both desire our best love to dear Papa, and to be kindly remembered to all our Uncles Aunts and Cousins, to Aunt Nabby, Miss H Trapp, to Miss Lydia who I am glad to hear keeps from the *lowpo*, our best thanks and respects are due to Uncle Robinson,[7] we also desire to be remembered to the Doctor, (Mrs Woolsey enquired about him and thanked him for remembering her.) to all our other good neighbors, I have not room to particularise, I hope Cousin William continues to get better, and am glad your little Betsey is so good, do you ever see John McCurdy, and how does Tom behave,[8] adieu dear Mama accept the best love of your grateful and affectionate Daughter

H TRUMBULL

7. Ichabod Robinson, the 81-year-old father of Miss Lydia Robinson. His sister, Faith Robinson, was the wife of Governor Jonathan Trumbull, Sr.

8. Mrs. Trumbull apparently acquired a Betsy as well as a Sylvia (p. 96, n. 1) during this year. In a letter written about 1805 Maria asked her mother to "remember me to Sylvia Betsey and the kitten," and later correspondence includes negotiations for the replacement of these girls. Tom was probably the current boy helper in the family, and John McCurdy a predecessor (very likely the 11-year-old illegitimate son of a Eunice Backus of Norwich who named John McCurdy, Hartford merchant, as the father).

*To Mrs. Trumbull at Lebanon*

New York [*Saturday*] 21 February 1801

MY DEAR MAMA

It is so long since I have written to you that I really fear you will think I have been negligent—which I certainly did not intend to be—but Harriet has been in such a writing humour of late—that she has taken all the business out of my Hands—I believe you have had our very important Journal down as late as wednesday—we were at home all the morning and the rain increased so much that it prevented our going to dancing school which to be sure was quite a disappointment—as we do love *some times* to dance a *little*—thursday morning Uncle Backus came to see us—and we went early to Mrs Sebors—from there to dancing school—from thence to drawing school and from there—to Mrs Coits where we drank tea and spent the evening with quite a large party—we were very much surprised to find Mr and Mrs Howland[1] there. However as they brought us letters why should not we be very much rejoiced too? and to be sure we were—we were attended home by Mr Lanman—who was very polite—indeed—the young gentlemen and one of the young ladies

1. Joseph Howland (1750–1836), father of Betsy and Joseph Howland, Mrs. George M. Woolsey, and Mrs. Levi Coit. He was one of Connecticut's most successful merchants, owner of a ship and fifteen or twenty brigs, schooners, and sloops. On this visit to New York he was arranging to buy Philipsburg (also called Philipse Manor) which was located in what is now Yonkers. The purchase (for $62,500) included 320 acres of land and 26 buildings, among them a manor house, inn, farm houses, and five mills (grain, plaster, lumber, and fulling). Howland moved his family there in the following spring but continued his Connecticut mercantile interests through a partner, Jesse Brown, Jr., of Norwich (p. 59, n. 8). As a business venture, Philipsburg was unsuccessful. It was sold at auction in 1813 for $56,000.

—had gone to a ball—and we set up till nearly three oclock expecting to have some fun, however—after all—we did not—and went to bed quite sleepy and tired—friday we spent at Mr Watsons and enjoyed ourselves rarely. We likewise called at Mrs Churches where we were recieved very cordially—tho' Mrs Church was gone to ride —but Miss Betsey was very polite indeed, and quite friendly. I suppose you have heared the melancholly news of Mr Jeffersons election, there was quite a rejoicing about and the cannons at the Battery were going as brisk as need be—and when we came home in the evening there was a large mob in the broad way made up of the very dregs of the town, and they to besure were fighting at a most terrible rate, however we got safe home at last—tho' we were not a *little* frightened—this morning I have been almost all over town a shopping with Mrs Sebor—and have got *things enough*—we went also to call upon Mrs Howland—and I dined at Mrs Sebors—Harriet was so much engaged with her music lesson that she could not go—from there I went to drawing school and am at last safe at home—to my great joy as I feel quite tired—Mr James Wadsworth has been to see us and John and I have been trying for an hour almost to cut Williams profile—and have at length succeeded—Harriet has gone to bed and I must bid you good bye my dear Mama for to night

Monday morning— —yesterday dear Mama we rose very early and went to the Battery to breakfast and from thence to Church with Maria [*Watson*]—where we had a very good sermon—we returned to Mr Watsons and set a little while to warm us—and get some wine and cake—we dined as usual at Mr Sebors—I was quite ill all day with the headache—however we made out to get twice to Church—we were attended home in the evening by Mr Eben Watson Mr Colt and Mr Phillips—so you see we had beaux plenty—this morning we have risen quite early—and have got through breakfast—Harriets Music Master has just gone—we are going to dancing school and to drink tea at Mrs Sebors—and now I believe I have got thro'

I have had since yesterday morning a strange kind of breaking out upon my hands and arms—and I am really quite frightened about it—when I got up yesterday—it was so early that the fires were not made—and tho' they got them a little kindled before we got away yet washing me and takeing such a long walk in the cold[2]—when I got to Mr Watsons and set down before a large fire in a very warm room my hands began to *burn and ache and itch,* and in a few minutes there came out all over them almost, great white blotches some of them as large as a quarter of a dollar—then they would go away and come again—and so it has been ever since—and I really begin to be quite frightened about it—they will swell up and ache most dreadfully—and you know Mama I am apt to conciet a little—and I am really affraid it is going to be *some thing else*—which you know would be shocking—and I can hardly take any comfort I keep thinking of it so—but however it will do no good to trouble you about it—as the matter will be determined before I can hear from you—Harriet has this minute recieved a letter from Sister—you asked dear Mama whether Lady Kitty smoked segars or pipes—she smokes segars tho I believe pipes are more fashionable as I see they have them at Mr Watsons—I

2. The temperature was sixteen degrees at 8:00 A.M. Laight Diary.

suppose you have heared of the famous duel between Mr James Wadsworth and Mr Cane—it is a thing I am sure I should never have thought of Mr Wadsworth—and I was so sorry I could have cried. He has been to see us once since but looked *quite down in the mouth,* and to think of thier going to Connecticut too![3]—Mr Cane shot *himself* in the foot—and they cannot extract the ball—and I am told he is very miserable—the ball entered at his knee and went down to his heel—I hope it will learn them not to be so wicked again—the young men here do so stand up for fighting duels that it makes me quite *mad*—one of them has fought a duel in his day and I must confess I dont think it much in his favour—but he declares he had rather *lose* his *life* than *submit* to an *insult.* What *nonsense*! Harriet has gone to dress herself to go out and I believe I must go too, pray remember me to all my Lebanon friends not forgetting in particular aunt Nabby Hyde and Miss Hannah Trapp—adieu dear Mama with best love to dear Papa from Harriet and myself I remain your truly greatfull and affectionate daughter

MARIA TRUMBULL

Harriet and myself wish very much to stay another quarter as we are very much engaged in our schools—and it will be quite a disadvantage to us to leave them

3. New Yorkers usually fought their duels across the river in New Jersey.

*To Mrs. Trumbull at Lebanon*

New York [*Monday*] 2d March 1801

DEAR MAMA

Mr Howland call'd at Mr Sebors yesterday, to tell us that he expected to leave town tomorrow and woul'd take letters or any thing else we wished to send, I fear'd I should not have time to write much, but the weather has been so unpleasant today as to prevent our going out, as we ought to have done, and afforded me more time, I think it is very probable that Mr Howland will not go so soon, they have staid now longer than they intended. We received last Monday a letter from Sister written at Lebanon; and thursday I had the pleasure of receiving a small one from Papa, and again on Saturday Maria received one from Sister at Hartford, I am very sorry Brother was so unwell while with you and hope he has by this time entirely recovered; the accounts Sister gives of my dear Mama's health being so much improved are very gratifying to us. We are both very well, and happy, tho' I think that both of us have had the Chicken Pox, but very light and without any inconvenience. I believe we must have been exposed to it one day when we were at Mrs Coits, she said her little girl was just recovering from it. I have not seen Mrs Howland since the afternoon she first came to town, I drank tea with her at Mrs Coits, I have call'd to see her but could not find her at home, Maria call'd the Saturday after with Mrs Sebor, who invited Mrs Howland and her children to drink tea with her the Monday following, and ask'd us to come also, Maria did, but I went with Maria Watson who urged me very much, to see Mrs William Woolsey, where we found Miss Pomeroy, and Miss Morgan, Tuesday it rained, but Miss Pell a friend of

Weltha's, was so good as to call with her, for us to go to drawing school in her carriage, we were to have drank tea with Mrs Fay, but the weather prevented our going, Wednesday morning Mrs Stewart call'd to see us with the Miss Barclays, daughters of the British Consul,[1] in the evening we were to go to Miss Murrays. Mr James Wadsworth call'd for us about eight, we found there a large party, had a charming ball, and a most elegant supper and came away a little before two, the Miss Murrays were very attentive and polite to every one, the Miss Churches, and Miss Barclays were there, and Mrs Hopkins, who is a charming woman, Thursday we went to dancing and drawing school. Friday we went to Mr Watsons, and in the evening to the play, which was tolerably entertaining,[2] we slept at Mr Watsons and staid till it was time to go to school, we drank tea at Mrs Stewarts. Mrs Sebor, Miss Barclay and Mr Beverly Robinson[3] were there, Sunday we went to Church, and call'd to see Mrs Adams[4] the late Presidents lady, but she was not at home. Mrs. Hopkins and the Miss Murrays call'd to see us while we were out, and Mr Wadsworth and Mr Mumford[5] in the evening. We have

1. Maria and Susan, daughters of Thomas Barclay, loyalist during the Revolution, who moved to Nova Scotia at its close. He returned to New York in 1799 when he was appointed consul. [142 Greenwich St.]

2. The program announced for February 27 was a comedy "WIVES AS THEY WERE, And Maids as they are" and a comic opera in three acts "THE CASTLE OF ANDALUSIA" written by John O'Keefe, Esq. *Mercantile Advertiser*, Feb. 26.

3. The 21-year-old cousin of Miss Barclay. He later married Frances Duer, and his brother Morris married Henrietta Duer.

4. Mrs. John Adams was returning from Washington to her home in Quincy, Mass.

5. Benjamin M. Mumford of Norwich, who had settled in New York around 1793. He was a 29-year-old bachelor in 1801, but married the following year.

been this Week past expecting Sally Colt and Rebecca Hopkins, as Weltha Morgan heard that they were coming on with Mr Terry,[6] Sister says in her last letter, that they are only waiting for an opportunity, so I imagine Mr Terry has not thought of coming. We were invited last week to dine at Mr Leffingwells, and to drink tea at Mrs Bradleys, but could not go, Mr Sebor has received a letter from Brother with some money, what he had I believe was nearly gone, for we have been getting some new gowns and things lately, I hope what he has now, will last till Mr Morgan comes. I was very much surprised at one of the reasons Papa gave for our perhaps not staying six months, I have heard no one here say a word of expecting any disturbances. People here seem quiet and peaceable enough. The democrats I believe are to have a procession and feast, on Wednesday, to testify their joy at Mr Jeffersons Election, but I have not heared much said of it: as for Papas other reason, I apprehend much more from that, and hope when he finds it inconvenient to keep us here any longer, he will send for us directly; but I wish to stay very much. My drawing master asked me how long we expected to stay, and upon my telling him "till June," he said he was very glad of that, for we should be able to do some handsome coloured peices; my music master too said the same, that I should be able to make considerable progress in that time; whereas if we return soon, we shall have to stop in our studies, just as we begin to improve, I believe you will think my dear Mama that we are very anxious to stay, but still I assure you, [*we*] wish very much to see all our friends, our dear Parents particularly. We have very warm pleasant

6. Nathaniel Terry (1768–1844), Hartford lawyer married to Catherine Wadsworth (sister of Faith's husband, Daniel).

weather for these some days past, it has been just like spring, I have [sat in my] chamber most all day without any fire, and have been sufficiently warm,[7] the roads I am told are very bad and I fear will prevent Sally's and Rebecca's coming on, I hope soon to hear my dear Mama of your being in Hartford with our dear Sister, where you will not feel our absence so much, and we shall hear oftener from you. I wish I could think of something pleasing to send you, but I have nothing but a great deal of love from Maria and myself to dear Papa and yourself. We both desire to be remembered to all our Lebanon friends, and neighbors, to Aunt Nabby Hyde and all our own family and believe me dear Mama your very grateful and affectionate daughter

HARRIET TRUMBULL

7. "Bull Frogs croaked—and Blue Birds chirrup'd this day," says the diary of Henry Laight for February 26.

*To Mrs. Trumbull at Lebanon*

New York [*Thursday*] March 5th 1801

My Dear Mama

Last monday after finishing my letter to you, Uncle Backus called to se us—he is really very kind and seems to feel quite interrested about us—he always enquires very particularly after the Lebanon friends, and I wish Mama that you would *all of you* send your *love* to him a little oftener, for it pleases him so when you do that I love to tell him—for he seems so sober here—that I quite pity him—tho' he appears to know *every* body yet I am tempted to believe that he dont care much for *any* body—I believe Harriet has told you of all our proceedings—until monday last—when we had quite a *procession* thro' our street[1]—there was a monstrous large ox all dressed with ribbons and flowers—and followed by such a *despicable rabble* as you never saw in *our* state—it was completely covered with *finery*—and really would have looked quite pretty upon any other occasion—
between its horns was a broad blue ribbon with Jefferson and Burr—written in [*torn*] letters and the poor creature was to be roasted whole upon the 4th of March—however they have since concluded to dispose of it in a better manner—and have cut it up and given it to the poor which I am heartily glad of, for now there has certainly one *good* thing been done, upon that *ugly day*—it was quite as large I believe as Uncle Trumbulls great ox—and it was one of the handsomest creatures I ever saw—Harriet and myself drank tea at Mrs Fays and found them very glad to see us—

1. The procession passed down Chambers St. probably because the ox was to be eaten by the inmates of the almshouse which was located there.

Tuesday morning we were out making calls—as it was a most beautiful day—we went to Mrs Johnsons Miss Murrays, Mrs Brunsons, and Mrs Sebors—and to drawing school, in the afternoon, we drank tea and spent the evening at Mrs Atkinsons—wednesday was a day of great rejoicing among the wicked ones—and the Bells were ringing—and the cannons fireing at the Battery all day like witches—in broad way—within sight of Col Burrs house there were no less than six flags out—and they had quite a grand procession and an oration—by a man who perjured himselfe a little while since—the vauxhall gardens were illumined and two figures of Jefferson and Burr—or the *triump of justice* and they had a new play at the African Theatre—Papa what *silly* fools the new Yorkers are—I quite glory in being a yankee[2]—we went to dancing school—and Mr

2. This was the day of President Jefferson's inauguration. The diary of Henry Laight records that all the church bells in the city rang except the Episcopal. According to contemporary newspapers, the procession marched up Broadway to the Brick Presbyterian Church where an oration was delivered by Tunis Wortman, a Republican lawyer and diligent party worker, whom the new administration rewarded with the post of clerk of the city of New York. The program also included a band concert, a reading of the Declaration of Independence, and a collection for the benefit of the poor. The procession then re-formed, returned by a different route to the Battery, and disbanded with the successive firing of 16-gun salutes from the cannons on the Battery, from the fort on Governor's Island, and from two warships in the harbor. The fireworks at the Vauxhall Gardens (an establishment for refreshments and entertainment in the outskirts of town, off Broadway) gave great offense to some of New York's Republican citizens "by making Jefferson and Burr discharge serpents, and representing them in *fire* of various colours; but this Mr. D. [*Delacroix*] done very innocently" said the Federalist *New York Gazette*. "He never dreamed of any unfavorable constructions being put upon his representations. It would have been well, however, if he had considered the difficulty of pleasing *such* an audience as were to be expected at *such* an exhibition."

Watson thought it was best for us to stay with them for the night as perhaps there might be some disturbance—however I believe there was none—only some *few* people were obliged to be *carted* home which I am apt to think is no uncomon thing upon such occasions—we are now at Mr Watsons—and I am writing on some dear soft paper—and with a nice pen of Mr Eben Watsons—who is one of the best young men in the world—I am sure, Mama that you would like him—Mr Watson and Maria desire love to Papa and Mama—O I had quite forgotten to tell you how wonderfully polite Mr Mumford was the other night at Miss Murrays—I danced with him several times, and he has since called to see us—Mr James Wadsworth poor man seems to feel quite dejected—and I really pity him very much—I cant find out what he has done—but the Watsons seem very much prejudiced against him—for my part I am hardly willing to believe that he has done any harm *intentionally* but strange things will happen—and I begin to think folks ant as good as I used to think them—I am sure they are not half as clever here as they are in Connecticut—they are so dissipated—and they swear—and get tipsey and every thing thats [wicked?]—I hope we shant learn any of thier *tricks*—and I think there is not much danger—for it puts me quite out of conciet to go *gadding* about—and I love to come here—where we dont hardly see a person all day—better than to go any where else—we visit very little indeed—and are very much engaged, so much so that we have little time to be idle—I have got partly thro' the second volume of Humes History of England—Lady Kitty has a great many Books—tho' we dont find much time to read as we go four times to dancing-school—three to drawing and Harriet takes a music lesson three times a week—we some times dont get our dinner at home more than once or twice in a fortnight—and I think we generally walk as much as four or five miles a day—we are going next monday to spend a *friendly* day with the Miss Murrays—for which however we are obliged to give up a *dancing day* but that is not much matter—Dear Mama you must excuse all the mistakes you find in this letter as Mr Watson and Eben have been talking as fast as need be—I hope Papa will find it convenient to let us stay another quarter—as it will really be a great pity to leave our schools now—I intend soon to send home my accounts—I have not bought one sugar plumb since I sent home the last—Harriet sends her best love—she has written to send by Mr Howland—pray my dear Mama give my very best love to all Uncle Trumbulls family and to Uncle Williams's, cousin William in particular who I hope by this time is quite well—remember me very respectfully to Uncle Robinson—my best love also to Miss Hannah Trapp[3] and aunt Nabby Hyde—tell the former that I hope we shall be able to show her some new fashions when we get home—and I hope to eat some of the latters nice cake—I have not seen any better since I have been here—my love also to Polly Williams and Polly Ely[4] when you see them and to Mary Fox—how does poor old Aunt Sarah do? tell her we have not forgotten her and Aunt Betty—and Old Betty Brown—we love them all—and pray Mama dont forget our own folks at home—I hope Miss Lydia Robinson feels in good spirits yet—give

3. Miss Hannah Trapp, so often remembered in these letters, was the local seamstress, who stayed with the Trumbulls when sewing for them.

4. The 17-year-old daughter of the Rev. Zebulon Ely (p. 28) and the 18-year-old daughter of Dr. Thomas Williams.

my love to her—I wont say a word of ugly cousin *Josey*[5] that starved the poor old [*torn*] horse (that I hope is yet alive and hearty) I hope that Mr and Mrs Lyman and Lydia[6] are well—tell cousin Jonathan[7] that I intend to write him very soon—I thank him a thousand times for his sweet letter—Mrs William Woolsey enquired very particularly after Doctor Clarcke—adieu my dearest Mama I remain with kind love to dear Papa your very greatfull and affectionate daughter

MARIA TRUMBULL

5. Joseph Trumbull, brother of cousins Abby and Sally, a senior at Yale and future governor of Connecticut.

6. William and Mary (Barker) Lyman of Lebanon, and their 19-year-old daughter.

7. The 11-year-old brother of Sally, Abby, and Joseph Trumbull.

*To Daniel Wadsworth at Hartford*

New York [*Friday*] March 6th 1801

Dear Brother

We had last evening the pleasure of receiving a long letter from you, and as the weather is so unpleasant as to confine us to the house, I take advantage of the leisure it affords me, to answer it immediately, and give you a great many thanks for writing to us, when your last letter has never been answered; but you, I am sure will have the goodness to excuse us, as you know how very much we are engaged, and how little time we have that we can write in. I am very sorry your visit at Lebanon should be rendered unpleasant by your illness. I hope when we receive letters again, to hear that you are quite recovered, and am proud that *my* currant Jelly, should be of so much service to you; what you mention of the state of politics at that time, accounts for a letter which I received from Papa and could hardly comprehend, as I could not see what politics could have to do with our staying here, he said that the confused and tumultous state he fear'd they would be in, would be a reason for our returning sooner than we wish'd,[1] people here appeared to apprehend no

1. Gov. Trumbull's letter was apparently written just before news of Jefferson's election reached Connecticut. He had recently received a letter from Connecticut Senator James Hillhouse in Washington informing him that "the Democrats are alarmed and threaten a dissolution of the union—and a breaking up of the government if they cannot have J[*efferson*]." Feb. 3, 1801, Jonathan Trumbull Correspondence I, Connecticut Historical Society. Trumbull may have been worried also by rumors of a Federalist conspiracy to continue the balloting stalemate in the House of Representatives until March 4 (the expiration of President Adams' term) and then vote to adjourn and let the Senate choose a president *pro tempore* (a Federalist of course) for the duration of the congressional recess. The New England Fed-

such danger, and we heard of no disturbances at Washington: last Wednesday the 4th of March, was a day of great rejoicings with the Democrats, they had a procession, and an oration delivered in one of the Churches, the bells were ringing and Canon firing great part of the day; we were out at dancing school, but did not return home, as there were so many disorderly creatures in the streets, that we were afraid to be out late, and we were advised by Mrs Sebor to accept of an invitation to sleep at Mr Watsons.

Mr Sebor told us several days ago, that he had received some money from you which should be ready for us whenever we call'd. I believe he had thirty dollars remaining of that, which you left with him. His family have been quite sick lately, all the Children have been ill with *Colds*, and Mrs Yates[2] little son has been and still continues very ill, I have not heard from him today, but I hope he is better, else I think they will be very much concerned about him.

I think Papa and Mama seem hardly willing to consent to our remaining here six months, but I hope we shall with Sister's and your assistance, be able to persuade them to agree to it; for I think that the three months yet to come will be of more advantage to us than those which are already past, and if we return soon it will take less time to forget what we have learnt, than it did to acquire it, and if

---

eralists would thereafter support the continuance of this man in office—by means of the New England militia if necessary. Such a coup might have caused civil war. *American Mercury*, Feb. 26, 1801.

2. Mrs. Adolphus Yates (Margaret Winthrop), the widowed sister of Mrs. Sebor, Mrs. Stewart, and Francis Bayard Winthrop, lived with the Sebors until August, when she married again.

we continue our studies, we shall I hope be able to pursue them alone at our return; Maria has got thro her drawing book, and is now on a board, as you may remember seeing some peices when you was in the schoolroom, with paper stretched tight on a board, as my book was larger than hers I have not finished it yet, but am to be on a board soon. I am much obliged to you for what you [*say*] concerning my music; I think Mr Hewitt seems to be much of your opinion. Since I have gone thro the first small book which he had given me, and contained simple pieces for new beginners, he has made it a practise to give me for one lesson a piece, and the next a song; and I [*find*] them all difficult enough, so much so that I can play none of them readily & easily, tho I find that the two or three first were the hardest, he has given me some peices that he has composed himself I suppose purposely for his scholars, he has made me sing once or twice, and began with raising my notes, but we have not advanced far, as I have had a cold.

We call'd last week to see Mrs Church, she had *really* gone to ride herself but the youngest Daughter [much agai]nst our inclination, received us very politely, we have heard nothing from them since,—but met the young Ladies at the Miss Murrays ball, they just spoke to us. We are so much engaged that we have very little time to visit, and can never dine out without giving up some school, as the only [*day*] which we have to ourselves we are engaged at Mr Watsons; I think we should sometime when invited to spend the day with people who have treated us with great attention, give up dancing, drawing we do not chuse to loose for any thing, Miss Murrays, asked us to come in a sociable way and spend a day with them, and as they have been very polite to us, we thought it best to give up our school; I wish you or Sister would tell us what we had best do on such occasions. We both desire a great deal of love to all friends at Hartford; particularly to Sister and yourself, from your gratefull and affectionate sister

Harriet Trumbull

*To Mrs. Trumbull at Lebanon*

New York [*Monday*] March the 8th [*9th*] 1801

My Dear Mama

I don't know how many letters you will recieve by Mrs Howland but as she keeps staying we must keep writing or our letters will be very old by the time you get them. I dont really think that Mrs Howland has done exactly right in not haveing once called to see us tho' she has been in town a great while—and the walking has been charming almost all the time—we have been very often to see her, but have generally found her out, and I think that among some of her rambles—she might have stopped a few minutes at our house, I dare say she has taken longer walks—however it is not much matter—so to begin my journal, last thursday after writeing to you from Mr Watsons—we went to Mr Sebors to dine—from thier to dancing and drawing school, and drank tea and supped at Lady Mary Watts's. Friday it rained and snowed very much which prevented our going to Mr Watsons—Saturday the walking was so bad that we thought it impossible to get to drawing school, however Miss Pell was so good as to call for us in her carriage. She is really a sweet girl and very kind to us—Sunday we were at Church all day and dined and drank tea as usual at Mr Sebors, we found Uncle Backus at home—[*he*] desires his love to you and all the Lebanon friends. This morning Harriet has just been takeing her Musick Lesson—and is now eating her breakfast—I send you a little scrap of our gowns, to see if you like them, Mrs Howland will be better able to tell you how they make gowns than I shall—I think the most fashionable way seems just as one pleases—I also send my account and two little drawings—I hope soon to be able to draw much better. Mrs Watson desires to be particularly remembered to the family,—adieu my dearest Mama I have got a long walk to take this morning and to dine out and am in a hurry with best love to dear Papa and all friends in which I am joined by Harriet I remain your very affectionate daughter

Maria Trumbull

*To Mrs. Trumbull at Lebanon*

New York [*Tuesday*] March 11th [*10th*] 1801

DEAR MAMA

I wrote you last week by Mrs Howland who expected to have gone then but was prevented by the badness of the roads from going till today, so that my letter will be very old by the time it reaches you, Maria however wrote a few lines yesterday, that you might know we were well; we saw Mr & Mrs Howland very little while they were in town, I am not willing to think it was any fault of ours, as we call'd to see them a number of times and could never but once find them at home; yet altho they were out so much, they neither of them had the goodness to call and see how we were situated which I was a little surprised at, as I thought they would wish to tell you that they had seen us at home, and how we looked, but I suppose they were more agreeably engaged. We had the pleasure of receiving two letters from you my dear Mama last Thursday, and one from Brother, he says he is much better himself, tho not quite recovered, and that they left you better, than he has seen you for some time, I am rejoiced to hear it, and hope & beg you will remain so Dear Mama, and keep up your spirits till we return, he says you appear'd willing we should stay, as long as [*we*] wish to; if Papa thinks he can without any great inconvenience support us here till June, I hope he will consent to, as it will be so much for our advantage. Weltha Morgans mama, writes her that she hears *we* wish to continue here till June, but she hopes *Weltha*, will, be *ready* to return the *first of May*; I suppose she thinks it is want of feeling in us to want to be absent from our friends, so long, but it is no such thing, I am sure we wish to see our Parents as much as weltha can hers, but we are anxious to have the advantages we enjoy, as long as we can: Maria sent you some of her drawings by Mrs Howland, I dare say you will think them pretty, but in one quarter more, we shall have some much superior to those, to shew.

We were very much surprised a few days ago, to meet Mr Sanford[1] in the streets, he had just then arrived and today call'd to see us, I think he looks better than when we saw him at New Haven, and he says he is, tho he took a violent cold coming here. Last Wednesday we went to dancing school and slept at Mr Watsons, for there were such rejoicings in honour of Jefferson, that we were almost afraid to be at home, as at our part of the town they are chiefly Democrats, and not very *reputable* people; but our fears were groundless, as every thing was quiet, Thursday we were at school again, and drank tea, spent the evening and supp'd, with Lady Kitty and the family, at Lady Mary Watts's; Friday it storm'd so much that we could not go to Mr Watsons and they could not send for us, Saturday, Miss Pell was again so kind as to take us to drawing school, Sunday we went to Church and to Mr Sebors, Monday we went to Mr Murray's to spend the day, and a charming day it was, Mr & Mrs Murray are very plain good people Mrs Murrays mother[2] who is an old quaker lady lives with them, and her brother, the young ladies are very amiable and accomplished, they all appear to wish to have us feel happy and at home there; we saw a great many of their drawings and they play'd and sung for us, the family

1. Probably Peleg Sanford who had business dealings with the Trumbulls for many years.

2. Mrs. James Lindley (Susanna Lownes) of Philadelphia.

move into the country early, and they say we must come and stay some days or a week with them, and that they will give us lessons in music and drawing, that we shall lose nothing by it, they sent us home in their carriage highly delighted with our visit. Today we have been at drawing school and drank tea at home.

Mr James Wadsworth has been fighting a second duel; with a brother of the gentleman he fought with before; and I am told is wounded in his leg, I have not heard particularly, but hope he is not badly hurt.[3] Poor Aunt Sarah! I am sorry she has so much illness, and am very much grieved to hear that Cousin William gets no better, I desire my love to him and all Aunt Williams's family. I want to see you very much dear Mama, and very often think what you are doing, the family is so regular that I am sure I often guess right; I hope sometimes that you are thinking of me at the same time, and can almost hear you wish of a Saturday night, that the girls had some of our "good baked beans," when I

3. The Bleeker diary records that the duel was fought with Oliver Kane (also spelled Cane and Caine) at Hoebuck, New Jersey, on the afternoon of March 9. Wadsworth was shot through both legs; his opponent was not touched. Oliver Kane was the brother of John and Elias Kane one of whom apparently fought the earlier duel with Wadsworth which may have been about a business matter. In 1795 the three brothers had been in business together as the firm John Kane & Co., and by 1801 they had three firms with overlapping membership. The Kane brothers' sister was the wife of Thomas Morris, son of Robert. Wadsworth had been agent for some of the Morris lands in the Genesee country, but in 1800 Robert Morris' huge holdings there were virtually wiped out by foreclosures to satisfy his creditors. One hundred thousand acres of his land went to John Barker Church, who was Wadsworth's second in the duel with Oliver Kane.

set and think of home I feel as if I could fly, but I have no leisure to be homesick.

I have a most wonderfully [*torn*] music master, he composes a great deal himself, and told me today he [intends to] publish some marches, and asking if my Papa was not Governor of Connecticut & said in compliment to me he would have one in honour of him; so I suppose when I return I shall be able to play "Governor Trumbull's March." I paid Lady Kitty several days ago 15 dollars; she has received in all 125 dollars, just her terms for three months, expired the 1st March, she desires not to be paid again till the 1st May. Uncle Backus call's to see us frequently, he always inquires after you and desires to be remembered to you. Has Papa received letters from Uncle John lately? there was a packet arrived here last week after a short passage, by which I hoped he would hear from him. Wee call'd at Mrs Churches some time ago, she was not at home, but her youngest Daughter received us very politely, tho at Miss Murray's ball, she told her that she was not acquainted with us; Mrs Church is gone to Albany to see her sister who has been very sick. Adieu, Dear Mama please to give my best love to Dear Papa, and remember me to Aunt Nabby and all our Lebanon friends and acquaintance, I remain your very grateful and affectionate Daughter

HARRIET TRUMBULL

Marias best love to Papa & Mama.

*To Mrs. Trumbull at Lebanon*

New York [*Wednesday*] March 18th 1801

My Dear Mama

How do you do at Lebanon and all the rest of the dear good friends? I do so long to see you all that I can hardly have patience to think that I am more than a hundred miles from you. It is a dreadful rainy evening—and I sit up here quite comfortless in my lonely chamber, listening to the deep howling of the wind that blows strong from the river—and the rain pelting against the window—Harriet has just come in and makes it a little more cheerfull but it has been a sad dull day—we have not once been out, nor have we seen any body the whole day—and to say the truth our feelings have corresponded a little with the weather without. However I dont know but it has served to make us a little more industrious—as we have been sitting by ourselves working and reading to each other all most all day—and as evening comes on we begin to *cheer up* as you know Mama we sometimes do at Lebanon after a dull day—I suppose by Mrs Howland you heared all our news—and I hope you were pleased with our gowns—I think the calico one remarkably pretty—and for the width and fineness remarkably cheap—it was I believe more than a yard wide and about four and tenpence our money—those dark blue calicos are the most fashionable now—we have not written you I believe since last wednesday since when not many very *memorable* events have taken place—however as we have the vanity to think that any thing relating to us will be interresting to you—I will I believe give you a short account of them—on wednesday evening we went to the play where we were tolerably entertained with a new thing that has just come out but as I know my dear Mama is not wonderfully fond of such things, I will not tire her with a description of it[1]—we returned to Mr Watsons where we spent the night—and slept three in a bed—thursday afternoon we drank tea and spent the evening with Miss Nanny Brown—friday as usual we spent at the Battery and were all *glad enough* to see our dear Sally Colt who came in upon us very unexpectedly—we drank tea at a Miss Fitches in Pearl Street[2]—all the family at home were gone to a party at Lady Mary Watts's and what we thought a little strange we alone out of the family were

1. *Abbé de l'Epée, or the Dumb Made Eloquent* was scheduled to have its second performance this evening but the morning papers carried a cancellation notice occasioned by bad reviews. Instead the management of the Park Theater presented two proven hits. Harriet and Maria saw *Abaellino, The Great Bandit,* a tragedy translated from the German by William Dunlap (Franz Kratter was presumed to be the author). When it was first performed in February the enthusiasm of the audience had been "so long and so loud as almost to border an uproar," and its continuing popularity was "testified by crouded audiences in the most tempestuous weather." According to one reviewer, the plot "partakes more of the truly sublime and of the sublimely mysterious than that of any piece within our recollection. At the end of the first act we should be apt to suppose that the author had gone to his utmost length: yet every act increases the interest and the last rises to a height almost unexampled. . . . The concluding act with respect to decoration and scenic effect, is the finest perhaps ever exhibited on our stage." The second piece of the evening, *Who's the Dupe,* a farce in two acts, had been equally well received, with special praise going to the actor Joseph Jefferson: "He is unquestionably the most uniformly chaste comedian our stage has ever possessed. Fully conscious of his power to display the meaning of the author, and draw forth the approbation of the discerning, he never descends to buffoonery or indecency to catch the worthless plaudits of the misjudging vulgar. We hope the little comedy will be repeated." *New-York Gazette,* Feb. 27; *Mercantile Advertiser,* Feb. 13, Mar. 5.

2. A daughter or niece of William Fitch, merchant. [336 Pearl St.]

left uninvited—however we were determined not to mind
it for it is not the first time, we have been so neglected
by them, and I really believe we enjoyed ourselves much
better as we stayed at Mr Watsons till near ten oclock and
then Roswell and Harry came home with us and stayed
till almost twelve—and I believe it is the first time since
we have been here that we have had any of our friends by
ourselves and undisturbed by the rest of the family—
Saturday was very rainy however we made out to get to
drawing school and I got me a dear little Hat—it cost two
dollars and a half—it is a spotted brown and white chip and
trimed with pink and white ribbons—Mrs Sebor
thought my other one was not fit to wear—we drank tea and
spent most of the evening at Mrs Sebors—they are indeed
some of the very best people in the world—Mrs Sebor in
particular seems to feel almost as much interrested in us as
if we were her children— she advises us what to do and
makes us feel as much at home as if it really was so—we
get our dinner there five times in the week and seldom miss
a day of being there once and some times two or three times
—I dont know how we shall ever repay her kindness.
Sunday we were at Church all day—in the evening we were
walking with Sally and the boys—they are charming
clever, Mama—I am sure you would like them both—I
hardly know which is best Roswell or Harry—we were out
a shopping all monday morning—and drank tea after going
to dancing school at Mrs Pattersons—tuesday we went
to drawing school as usual and drank tea and spent the
evening at General Stevens's with a large party—we were
attended home by our good Harry—and found Uncle
Backus—sitting very quietly by the fire side waiting for
us—tho' it was nearly ten oclock—he had indeed his

sitting breeches on and I did not know as he ever would have gone—I am almost sure he was asleep a good deal of the time and I am sure we had hard work to keep our eyes open—at length about half past eleven he motioned to go—and glad was I—for tho' he is a clever man and our good Uncle yet we dont know what to say to him—especially when he stays so for ever—to day we have been sitting as I told you before quite alone and not in very good spirits—here sits Harriet gapeing away like every thing and I must stop a minute and laugh at her— — —and now I believe I have got through my journal—I suppose Mama you have heared of Mr James Wadsworths second duel—I believe you will think the old cat is in the man—but I think from all account that even this is not likely to be the last—poor man I fear he has got into a bad scrape tho' we have not yet been able to learn what he has done only they say he is a *"damned rascal"* —a dreadfull hard name I think! I really can not help loveing and respecting him—and I dont at all believe that he is a bad man—I think there must be some mistake about it. He talks of going to Hartford very soon, I suppose when he has got quite well—we have only seen him once since the last duel—he was but slightly wounded —in *both* legs—I think Mr Kane must be an excellent marksman— —

Harriet bids me have done soon as she is quite tired of seeing me write—she sends her best love and to all friends —remember me also very affectionately to every body *dear dear* Papa in particular and dont forget Aunt Nabby Hyde—we do long to see you all dreadfully—adieu my dearest Mama accept a *very very* great share of love from your very gratefull and affectionate daughter

Maria Trumbull

*To Mrs. Trumbull at Lebanon*

New York [*Thursday*] March 26th 1801

DEAR MAMA

It is a long time indeed since I have written to you and I fear you will think me a sad girl; but I am sure if you knew how much I have been hurried and engaged, you *could* not be angry with me, I intend now to write a long letter, and let you know some of the many things that I have been doing. We received your letter last thursday, directed for us both, how happy it is that we can so often have the pleasure of hearing from you, I dont know what we should do without letters from home; Sister wrote me that Papa talk'd of going to Hartford last week, and of your going with him, but I think if the weather was as wet and disagreeable with you, as it was here, you did not go then, I hope if you are not already there, you will go soon and make a long visit; I wish we may find you there when we return, as I suppose it will be while the Assembly is sitting, and (if the Democrats do not succeed in their schemes) Papa will be there, and it will be very pleasant to find all our friends together in the same place we left them; have you yet laid any plan for getting us home? we begin to think of it a little, but hope you have given up the idea of our returning with Mr & Mrs Morgan, they are coming so soon, Weltha is very happy expecting them next week, how I wish my Papa and Mama would come for us; Sally Colt says that you talk'd of comeing, and returning with us by the way of Rome;[1] but I suppose it was all talk, and nothing else. We were very much rejoiced

1. The Trumbulls had friends (Colts), relatives (Huntingtons), and probably business around Rome, New York, which had been settled largely by Connecticut people.

at seeing Sally, we were at Mr Watsons, she opened the door softly, and came in upon us very unexpectedly; what was very provoking was, that we were all engaged to drink tea with Miss Fitch, and Mrs Watson thought it was necessary for us to go, and as [*she*] went out herself, we were obliged to leave Sally alone, but we returned very early and spent the evening with her, and then call'd to see Rebecca Hopkins, Saturday morning we were out together, it was a very unpleasant day, we went to drawing school in the afternoon, and drank tea at Mrs Sebors, Sunday we went to church, dined with Mrs Sebor, and in the evening Sally and Roswell Colt, and Harry Hudson, call'd for us, we went to Mr Brunsons to see Rebecca,[2] Monday I took a music lesson, and we were out all the morning in pursuit of a bonnet but did not find one, we call'd to see Mrs Leffingwell and went to dancing school, and to drink tea with Lady Kitty and the family at Mr Patersons,[3] the Miss Ivers[4] had sent for us to go there, Teusday we went to Drawing school, and to General Stevens's to tea, they had a good deal of company, Mrs Fay, Miss Broome, Miss Hopkins, Miss Watson, Miss Colt, Miss Morgan, and several others, Wednesday we were kept at home by the weather which was very bad, Thursday we were invited to drink tea with Mrs Bradley, but as we did not wish to go, and were advised

2. Rebecca Hopkins (1782–1803), daughter of Dr. Lemuel Hopkins of Hartford, was staying with the Brunsons to whom she was related by several marriage ties.

3. John W. Patterson, whose wife was a cousin of Lady Kitty's. [136 Pearl St.]

4. Boquet (age 15) and Eliza (age 18), daughters of Hezekiah Beach Ivers (1749–1795), a rope manufacturer, who moved to New York from Stratford before the Revolution.

by Lady Kitty, and several of our friends not to;[5] we pleaded a prior engagement to Miss Watson. We went to dancing and drawing schools, and drank tea at Mr Watson. It rain'd in the evening, but we walked home attended by Roswell, and Harry, Friday the weather was so unpleasant that we hesitated about going out, but as it did not absolutely rain, we ventured to go to Mr Watsons, the Major [*James Wadsworth*] dined there, we got home in the evening, just before it began to rain, Saturday morning was very wet, but as it cleared up a little at noon, we went to drawing school, and to drink tea with Sally Colt at Mrs Fay's, Sunday it almost rain'd but we went to Church, and spent the day at Mrs Sebors I beleive we have miss'd but two Sunday's since we have been in New York of going to church, both forenoon, and afternoon, Monday morning it rain'd and clearing up, we went with Mr Eben Watson and Harry Hudson, to see *sights*, the *invisible woman*,[6] and the *learned pig*, we

5. Probably Mrs. Walter Bradley, whose Republican husband was later appointed United States revenue collector at Fairfield, Conn. She was a New Haven girl and would almost certainly have known Mrs. Fay, who also came from there and who also had Republican connections—not very common in Connecticut. It was only at Mrs. Fay's house that Harriet and Maria ever encountered Mrs. Bradley. Their social snubbing of the lady may mean that they had just heard of some particular maneuver by her husband in the Republican campaign to oust Governor Trumbull and the rest of the Federalist establishment in Connecticut.

6. "The invisible woman," a phenomenon which had been exhibited in France, could be seen for fifty cents at a house on William St. An advertisement in the *Mercantile Advertiser* (March 3) announced that

> the habitation of the INVISIBLE WOMAN, is a box about five feet long and one foot square, glazed with glass, so that the view of the spectators is clear all through, it is suspended by a small rope and perfectly isolated, from thence she answers any questions put to

went to dancing school, and to drink tea with Sally Colt at Mrs Leffingwell's, and all went with her to the play,[7] with Mr E Watson, Roswell and Harry, for our gallants, Becca Hopkins and Weltha Mo[*rgan*] were there with Mrs Brunson, Teusday Morning we went out with Sally, to drawing school in the afternoon, and drank tea at Mr Littles, they asked us to dine there one Sunday before, but we were engaged, they were all well, and very polite to us, and we had a pleasant visit, they live very prettily, and are going to move this spring into a house he has been building; we came home pretty early, that I might learn my music lesson, and write, Mr Watson and Mr Colt came to see us, and I only learnt my music after they went away.
Wednesday morning I took a music lesson, and went to Mrs Fays, with Sally to make us some bonnets after one Miss Broome had; Maria and myself dined and spent the

---

> her by the spectator. She will mention the form or colour of anything presented to her. She whistles, blows, and does not differ in any degree from another person but by her invisibility.

Another description in the *Daily Advertiser* (March 21) explained that the

> answers seem to come from *within* the transparent box and in a female voice, they are full of pleasantry and intelligence and in a French accent—This effect is produced some say by ventriloquism, others, with more probability, by an artificial propagation of sound as in the case of the speaking figure now exhibiting by Falconi in Baltimore.—But in the present instance the mode which has been adopted is so ingeniously veiled as hitherto to elude all discovery.

7. The program on March 23 included *The Honest Thieves*, a farce in two acts, and *Peru Reveng'd, or the Death of Pizarro*, a tragedy by Kotzebue which used the elaborate scenery that had been painted for *The Virgin of the Sun* and for *Pizarro in Peru, or the Death of Rolla*. The last two were other Kotzebue plays on the Peruvian theme that were presented earlier in the season (p. 40).

day with Mrs Coit, afterwards, Weltha, and a Miss Van Wyke were th[ere?] Becca H, Sally, and Maria Watson, with several other ladies and gentlemen [*were expected*] but were all prevented by the rain, except, a german Mr Thies, [Mr       ], Mr Colt and Mr Hudson. Today it rains and snows by turns, and [*I*] fear we shall not be able to go to drawing school, unless Miss Pell should call for us; I hope we shall have some pleasant weather, again, before we go home; we have a great many calls that ought to have been returned before this and when it has done raining we must go out. We are expecting to hear from you this evening my dear Mama, I hope we shall have good news, it is a long time since we have had a letter from dear Papa, we should be very glad if he would write, I suppose he is much taken up with politics. There is great news lately arrived in town from England,[8] but he will doubtless hear it before you get my letter; it is almost time for fremans meeting,[9] I shall want to hear the news then. I desire a great deal of love to Papa, and to be kindly remembered to all our friends and neighbors, to Cousin Harriet Elderkin[10] in particular, and believe me dear Mama your grateful and affectionate Daughter

HARRIET T

8. The ship *Liberty* had just arrived in 39 days from Liverpool bearing news from London up to February 9. Most newspapers featured a change in the British ministry as the most important item because "the change of *men* at the head of the British administration . . . may, probably, lead to a general peace." An armistice between France and Austria was also reported. *New-York Gazette*, March 24, 1801.

9. On April 13 each town in Connecticut would hold a "freemans meeting" to vote for town, state, and national officers.

10. Daughter (b.1768) of Col. Jedediah Elderkin of Windham. She was probably visiting either the Trumbulls or the Huntingtons.

*To Mrs. Trumbull at Hartford*

New York [*Thursday*] April 2d 1801

MY DEAR MAMA

I can assure you that we are very happy to direct our letters once more to *Mama in Hartford*, I suppose Lebanon is in all the majesty of mud just at present —and of course not very agreeable—prehaps less gay than ever—notwithstanding—I should like much to see it again —you need not fear our getting to [*too*] much attached to New York. I think there is no great danger—for—with all its gaities—it is not as good as Hartford and good old Lebanon—and I don't think people are very happy here, but to proceed to our journal—which I suppose you all find very interresting—I believe we have not written since last sunday evening[1] which was gloomy enough I am sure—I never saw a darker night—and it so *eclipsed* the *eclipse* [*of the moon*] that we could not se it at all—monday tho' it was not very pleasant I made out to get to dancing school and back again tho' to be sure I was in a pretty pickle—I had to change all my cloathes—which was a great pity as they were clean—tuesday we went to drawing school from whence I went to Mr Sebors and from there to the Ball[2]—which was really quite splendid it was in the new assembly room—and there was a great many people—and very elegantly dressed—I had the pleasure of dancing with Mr Mumford who is really very polite indeed—he was quite *my beaux* all the evening—and attended us home—and the next morning he called to see us—I am afraid he thinks

1. This letter is missing.

2. M. Lalliet, a New York dancing master, gave the ball for his "scholars and friends" at the City Hotel on Broadway. The price of admission was one dollar. Maria's attendance with the Sebors suggests that she and Harriet and Eliza Sebor were pupils of M. Lalliet.

me a great fool—for I am so unused to hearing fine things that the only reply I know how to make is either to hang down my head in silence and feel as ashamed as a dog—or else to look all around the room and begin to talk of something else as fast as ever I can—I really like him very well—he seems a very good natured clever man—but he dont know how to treat little girls—that is certain—I slept at Mrs Sebors—Harriet did not go to the Ball—and spent the evening at Mr Watsons—wednesday morning we went to call at Miss Harts—and Mr Watsons—we dined and spent the day at Mr William Woolseys—we went in the evening with Sally Colt, Roswell and Harry to se Rebecca Hopkins—this morning I have been to ride in a *gig* with Harry Hudson—we set out a little after six had a charming ride of *fourteen* miles[3] and returned to breakfast—it is a lovely day as need to be—Harriet has gone to Miss Murrays—and it is almost time I was dressing me for dancing school—we are going to drink tea with Mrs Leffingwell—

We have not seen Uncle Backus these three weeks—and so have had no opportunity of delivering your messages—you mentioned Mama in one of your letters—my leaving of [*off*] reading to Lady Stirling—it is because I dont mention it, for I read to her very often—Sally Colt desires to be particularly remembered to all the dear friends, do my dear Mama make as long a visit as you can at Hartford—I am

3. Maria and Henry Hudson probably took "the fourteen mile round," a favorite pleasure drive of New Yorkers that crossed a "kissing bridge" where tradition entitled Henry to collect a toll. The route went out the east side of Manhattan by the Boston Road, cutting diagonally across what is now Central Park from north of 91st St. toward 115th St., and returned on the Hudson side of the island by the Bloomingdale Rd., roughly parallel to present-day Broadway.

sure you must enjoy yourself much better there than at Lebanon—we look forward with much pleasure to the time of our return—give my very best love to the dear good family I do long to see you all very much indeed—I hope cousin Sally enjoys herself finely at Hartford give my kind love to her—adieu my dear Mama excuse the shortness of this as I am in great haste I remain your gratefull and affectionate daughter

MARIA TRUMBULL

*To Mrs. Trumbull at Hartford*

New York [*Saturday*] April 4th 1801

DEAR MAMA

We received your letter last Teusday, and were very happy to see by the date of it that you were again in Hartford where I hope you will remain some time; Maria wrote to you one day this week, and hearing the Major was going soon and would call on us to take letters, kept her letter, but he has not call'd yet, and the letter will be pretty old before you receive it. I have executed your commission about the bonnet, but I fear it will not please you; I look'd almost every where for black chips and found none except like what I send, only very small ones, with Sally Colts advice I purchased this, I thought if it was not quite large enough you could let it out behind, and if after all it would not answer, you might put [*it*] in some of our shops at Lebanon, the price of it was two dollars, I shall endeavour to send it as soon as possible, and have put in [*the*] box some things from Sally Colt, for Mary.[1] I will try to find some hair such as you want but think it will not be possible to get any thing at the price you mention. Weltha Morgan expects her Parents next week, I wish I could see mine as soon; I am very sorry dear Mama that you should [*think*] our home will not seem as pleasant to us at return; I believe on the contrary that we shall love it the more for our visit to New York. I wish instead of short journeys about home, you would consent to come on here, and I hope we shall be able to persuade you to come on for us;

1. Mary, the 13-year-old sister of Sally and Roswell Colt was staying in Hartford with Col. and Mrs. Jeremiah Wadsworth (parents of brother Daniel). The Colt family had other daughters named Harriet Wadsworth and Catherine Wadsworth (after Daniel's sisters). The Fay family also named a daughter Harriet Wadsworth.

if Papa should be elected again, after the session of the assembly, it would be a charming time to travel and we should be just ready to return, do think, and talk of it Dear Mama and put in execution, *you* never was in New York, and Papa I am sure would be very happy to see his friends here, Mr Watson asks us often if you dont think of it, and wishes you would come, he wants to know he says if you intend it. Papa asks if we did not leave the Children of the Abbey[2] at home; it is in the *little desk* of mine in the *library, the key of which* I gave you. We send home in your band box, some more of our drawings, those Mrs Howland carried were done by Maria. Mama I wish you would get Aunt Wadsworth to let Mary Colt make you a visit this spring, her brother proposed it to me, as he supposed you was much alone. I obtained Sally's consent for it, and a promise to write on to Mary that she might go when you ask'd her: I think if you should be at Lebanon to stay again before we return, it will give you pleasure to have her with you. I have not time to add more than our best love to Papa Brother and Sister, and all friends. I will write again as soon as I can dear Mama your gratefull and affectionate Daughter

HARRIET TRUMBULL

2. A four-volume tale by Regina Maria Roche (1764?–1845) already in its fourth English edition within as many years. Although hilariously sentimental and florid to modern ears, it was relished throughout the nineteenth century and given numerous American printings.

*To Mrs. Trumbull at Hartford*

New York [*Tuesday*] 7th April 1801

My Dear Mama

Altho' I wrote this morning to Sister yet as I have another so good opportunity again by the Major, I thought I would improve it—as prehaps I may not have such an one again this long time—I hope the Major will not lose it—as that would be almost as bad as not to go—we have been to drawing school this afternoon—and since then to Mr Watson. We found the family just at tea when we got home, and Miss Brown with them—she has just gone—Harriet is practicing, the children studying their lessons—and the room is remarkably still for a wonder—and if I had any thing in the world to say, this would be an excellent time and I would write my Dear Mama a very long letter,[1] but upon my word I feel so stupid that I can hardly move my pen—and when it does move, it seems to produce nothing worth reading—we have heared by Mrs. Morgan a kind of flying report of all the barns being burnt at Hartford—we hardly know whither to believe it or not, but I think if it is true you must have been very much alarmed indeed—I think they must have been set on fire by some ill natured person and it was a great favour that the flames spread no farther—I hope to hear very soon whither it is true or not[2]—we were very

1. Maria must have written the journal for the preceding four days in the above mentioned letter to Faith who, she knew, would show it to her mother.

2. The *Republican Watch-Tower* of April 10 reported that in Hartford on Friday, April 3, a fire of incendiary origin consumed the barns of the Rev. Strong, Nathaniel Terry, and Judge Ellsworth and that another belonging to Col. Wadsworth was pulled down to prevent the fire from spreading. Had the evening not been very calm, it was said, a major part of the city would have been destroyed.

glad indeed to hear that Papa had bought that house of Mr Morgans—I really hope you will be tempted some time or other to move up there—we should all be so glad and I am sure Mama you would enjoy yourself much better to be so near Sister—I have been interrupted by the entrance of Mr James Wadsworth who I believe will be the bearer of this letter after all as he says he is certainly going tomorrow in the Stage and has engaged a seat so I hope the driver will make him pay damages if he dont go—he is a dear good man and I love him dearly—but positively I have nothing to say and so with my best love to dear Papa and all friends I remain your sincerely affectionate daughter

Maria Trumbull

*To Mrs. Trumbull at Lebanon*

New York [*Thursday*] April 9th 1801

Dear Mama

I wrote you a short letter last Saturday and put it in the box with the bonnet and other things, the gentleman who took charge of it, Mr Phillips, did not go as soon as he expected, so that the letter will be quite old before it reaches you, and as I suppose you did not receive the last one before that, because I directed it to Lebanon; you will think I have quite given up writing; it is a long time since we have had a line from you or Papa, more than a week; but in that time we have received several from brother & Sister. We were very much astonished at one piece of intelligence brother gave us that Papa had purchased Mr Morgans house, we have been wondering what has happened that he has grown so rich of a sudden as to buy that house and give me a piano forte, we almost concluded that he must have drawn the highest prize in some lottery;[1] and ventured on the strength of the supposition, to get a dollars worth of cake sugarplumbs and figs; I was so rejoiced to hear the news, that tho it was Sunday I could scarcely refrain from dancing and singing; and I told all my friends that "I was going to have a piano forte;" as Maria used to tell everybody *"we have got some ducks"*. I am a thousand times obliged to Papa, and only hope I shall not give him occasion, by negligence and inattention, to repent of his indulgence. Brother says Papa has no intention

1. The prejudices of Connecticut people did not extend to lotteries. These were government licensed for worthwhile public purposes such as constructing a road or bridge or rebuilding a church that had been destroyed by fire.

to remove to Hartford at present if ever, every body I know here is asking if we have heard of his purchase, and seem determined that he must go there to live, I think it would be an excellent plan, tho I should be very sorry indeed to leave Lebanon. How fortunate that our new house should escape, in the fire! I think you must all have been terribly frightened dear Mama, and very thankful that there was no more injury done by it. Mrs Morgan arrived in town last Sunday, Weltha was not very well, and I dare say for that reason was the more rejoiced to see her Mama, they expect Mr Morgan next week when they will begin to think of returning. Mrs. Morgan says you told her nothing but your ill health prevented your coming on here, I think that is one of the greatest reasons for your coming, as the journey would I daresay be of service to you, and the novelty of scene you would find here, would amuse you, I wish I could see you as I think I could more easily persuade you, than by writing, I am very much engaged about it indeed and it would be delightful if in June, Papa and you, Brother & Sister would take a carriage and come on for us; I can see no objection that could possibly be made to such a scheme, especially by you or Papa for I dont know any body that can leave home better; you never was here dear Mama, and therefore must wish to come, and it is so long since Papa was here, that he must surely wish to see his friends, and besides every other inducement (and I think there are a great many) it will be so gratifying to our *Pride*: indeed indeed the plan appears every way so excellent to me, that I think you cant refuse your consent to it. Sally Colt went last week to New Ark, with her friend Miss Boudinot,[2] who came over for her; we felt as if we had lost the best friend we had here when she left us. Fanny Leffingwell[3] is in town, there are really a great many of our acquaintances and friends assembled here, Rebecca is very well, and (I beleive) happy; she is much admired; she desired me to remember her best love always when I wrote home. I hope you will have [*a*] pleasant journey to Woodstock,[4] and return better and determined to think seriously and well of my New York plan, and find yourself in June ready and willing to put it in execution. I beg you would not be uneasy Mama on account of our dineing so often at Mr Sebors, we used only to eat some little at the side table with Eliza, because our school went in so early, and Mrs Sebor said it was no trouble, but we have done with it now, for the school does not begin till three so that we have time to dine at home. I believe I must close my letter as I have one to write to Brother, and by time I have finished that, it will [*be*] necessary that I dress to go out. With a great deal of love to Papa, and all friends, I remain dear Mama your grateful and affectionate

HARRIET TRUMBULL

2. Sally Colt for many years visited and corresponded with Catherine Boudinot (daughter of Elisha) who lived in Newark, N.J.

3. From Norwich; 18-year-old sister of William Leffingwell with whom she doubtless stayed.

4. Mrs. Trumbull was probably going to visit a cousin, Faith Williams, who had married John McClellan of Woodstock.

*To Mrs. Trumbull at Lebanon*

New York [*Thursday*] April 16th 1801

My Dear Mama

If you all think that we are bewitched, I can assure you it is no more than we think of you, for we have not recieved a single line from any of you since last friday which will be a week tomorrow and which seems almost an age to us—the reason you have heared from us so seldom of late—is that we have written by private opportunities, which have most of them disappointed us and I suppose some of the letters have not yet reached you which you ought to have had a week ago—last friday as usual we spent at Mr Watsons—Papas friend Mr Pickering was there—we had our old beaux Harry and Roswell to attend us home—the wind was amazingly high and if it had been in the right direction I dont know but [*it*] would have blown us as far as Lebanon—I am sure it was strong enough—however we had fine fun—saturday after drawing school we drank tea and spent the evening at Mrs Brunsons—Sunday we were at Church all day and dined as usual at Mrs Sebors—we spent the evening with Rebecca at Mrs Brunsons—poor girl! she little thought what a misfortune awaited her; she was in fine spirits and promised certainly to come and see us monday evening. Monday we dined at Mrs Sebors and went from there to dancing school—we were very much surprised when Harry came in the evening without Rebecca and equally grieved when we learnt the reason—I cant help thinking that her friends did very wrong to keep it from her so—for it came so very unexpectedly that it almost killed her[1]—

1. Rebecca had apparently not been informed of the serious illness of her father, Dr. Lemuel Hopkins, who died on April 14. A few hours

tuesday morning I went a shopping with Maria Watson and got me a cheap gown—it was very fine yard and a half wide muslin for seven shillings—or 5 and 3 our money—muslins are wonderfully cheap now—Fanny Leffingwell got a gown the other day for two dollars and a half—We drank tea at Mr Glovers with Wealthy—and had a mighty stiff prim visit—we spent part of the evening at Mr Watsons—yesterday after dancing School we drank tea at Mrs George Woolseys—and this morning I was up a few minutes after sunrise and am writing with the window open, I suppose there are not three people in the house up but Harriet and myself—and very probably some of the family *wont be* up these two hours—it is *sorrowfull* to think how much time they lose in bed—tho' the mornings are so long now yet we *very seldom indeed* get our breakfast before nine oclock; often till much later—and then as likely as not—not more than four or five of us sit down together—it quite puts me out of conciet of laying in bed and I do believe when I get home that I shall be up ever so early *scrubbing around* like any thing—for I have got to consider a clean house and *clean things* in it as one of the greatest *luxurys* in the world—and I am sure I never shall find fault again with any ones cleaning as much as they please—for my part I should really think it a great favour if I might have a broome and a dusting cloth—and a tub of water into the bargain to wash the knifes and forks and

---

before his death her uncle wrote a letter saying "Rebecca has not yet returned from New York; they sent for her on Saturday. She probably will not arrive until to-morrow evening, too late to see her father alive, though he has manifested strong desire that she might arrive before his exit." Quoted in Gurdon W. Russell, *Early Medicine and Early Medical Men in Connecticut* (Hartford, 1892) p. 87.

plates—but however dont be uneasy about us dear Mama for it will learn us not to be difficult—I have almost got over my squeamishness—and it is only on very extraordinary occasions that I am *annoyed* by it—I do some times it is true (when Lady Kittys face is turned) *soil* a clean table cloth by wipeing my knife—but that is a trifle—you know.

Mama what charming weather we have, I should think it would quite drive away your heighpo—but positively there is such a refreshing smell of broiled shad comes in at the window and *creates* such a gnawing in my stomach, that if I write any more I am sure I shall grow cross—and I must bid you adieu with best love to dearest Papa and all friends I remain your very affectionate daughter

Maria Trumbull

*To Mrs. Trumbull at Lebanon*

New York [*Friday*] 24th of April 1801

MY DEAR MAMA

We send you by Mr Taintor[1] the little *wig* you desired us to get, I hope it will please you, tho I am afraid at first sight you will be apt to think it *too* dressy—but indeed Mama it is not half as much so, as ladies of your age wear them—and I am sure not too much so for you—the curls which I suppose will frighten you most will all comb out—and I dare say you can make it look as old fashioned as you please—I only fear that the hair is a little too dark—but that is not of much consequence—and you will be quite sure of not being taken for a lady of *fashion*, as they wear white *hair* altogather now, and there can be nothing *less tonish* than a black wig—I think it is one of the best I have seen, and very proper for you and pray Mama dont go to imagine—that you cant wear it because it will make you look too young, for I can assure you it will have no such effect—it cost three dollars which was quite cheap—at least not dear—Lady Kitty is going to get herself a light coloured one—and she is but two or three years younger than you, and not a bit more fashionable, so Mama I am sure you can make no *reasonable objection* ———

Harriet wrote yesterday to you by the post,[2] of course I have not much to say at least not much news—this morning Mr Morgan came to see us before breakfast—and since breakfast Mr Lambert has done us the honour to call—Harriets music master has not been this week, he does indeed treat her very shabily—to day is friday, but as it

1. John Taintor, a Lebanon merchant.

2. This missing letter apparently contained the journal for the preceding week.

rains and they dont chuse to send for us at the Battery, why we content ourselves as well as we can to stay at home—I have not been in to the house since last friday—and I declare unless a carriage comes for us to day that I wont go there again untill next friday—for the old Lady promised when she asked us to come that when ever it rained they would send the carriage and I dont know how she can set her conscience at rest without—

O Mama you have no idea how I long to be at home I declare I can hardly content my self to stay six long weeks more—it does seem to me that it will feel so clever to be at home and live quiet once again and not see any body in a month—but just our good friends and neighbours—and all set around the tea table so comfortably—and have Mr Ely[3] or Doctor Thad or aunt Betty or some of the sober clever folks come in and enjoy themselves drinking a good dish of tea and some nice cake—without any ceremony or formality—O it will feel so good—I declare I feel all in a nestle when I think of it I do so long for the time to come—pray give my very best love to dear Papa and all friends aunt Nabby Hyde in particular and believe me your sincerely affectionate & dutifull Child

MARIA TRUMBULL

3. The Rev. Zebulon Ely (1759–1824), Lebanon minister for 42 years.

[*Probably enclosed with the preceding letter*]

[*New York Friday April 24 1801*]

Dear Mama

It rains so that we are prevented going to Mr Watts's [*she meant Watson's*], for we could not walk and they did not send their carriage; I have therefore time to write a few words, which in my haste I forgot to put in my letter, I shall send by Mr Morgan a cap crown which I have been working for Aunt Nabby Hyde, it has little merit, but has taken me some time to do it as I have but little time to work in, I beg she will accept it with my best love, if I was at home she should not receive it in such a condition, without being wash'd, or with out borders, but as it is highly probable I think, that she will not wear it this winter, I will make her some borders against I get home. I will endeavour to get the pieces of china, the first opportunity, Brother advised us not to go out a shopping alone, as we should be so liable to be cheated, but Mrs Sebor has been so good as to offer to go out with us at any time, as it is very seldom convenient for Lady Kitty to go; but I will thank you Mama, to send me a list of the pieces you wish for, as I may not be able to recollect all of them; any thing else that you or any of our friends may want we will get with pleasure. Adieu dear Mama please to give my love to every body that remembers me at Lebanon, particularly to Uncle Trumbull's, Uncle Williams's and Aunt Nabby Duttons families, to Miss Betty Miss Hannah, Miss Lydia R, Mrs Hyde and every body that enquires after us and believe me dear Mama your gratefull

Harriet

New York [*Thursday*] 7th May 1801

My Dear Papa And Mama

Mr Lanman call'd to see us a few evenings since, and brought us a letter from you, which Docter Pierce gave him, as he was too great an invalid to take so long a walk to bring it, we were very glad indeed to hear from you, as we had not received a line since General Huntington[1] came, and began almost to think that you had forgotten us, we have been so long absent; I think you must have call'd us rather negligent, as our letters are so long reaching you,[2] Mr & Mrs Morgan have returned, and without Weltha, much to the surprise of all their acquaintance I dare say, she is to return with us I beleive, which I suppose, and hope will be pretty soon. As the weather grows warm it is unpleasant in the city, we feel more and more desirous every day of seeing all our dear friends, and of again seeing Connecticut, but as to what Maria wrote, it was a whim of hers, our best friends, Mr and Mrs Sebor in particular, treat us with if possible more kindness and affection, and I hope we shall ever feel grateful to them. We are at their house a great deal and always appear to be welcome visitors, we intend to persuade Mrs Sebor to let Eliza return with us or make us a visit when they come to Middletown,[3] she is a fine girl. I wish Mama may

1. Jedediah Huntington (1743–1818), merchant, brigadier general in the Continental Army, and United States revenue collector at the port of New London, Conn. His first wife was a sister of Governor Trumbull. Although she died in 1775 and he remarried, the two families remained close.

2. This letter, too, was slow in reaching Lebanon. An outside endorsement on it notes additional postal charges and "Litchfield Missent & forwarded."

3. The Sebors had relatives in Middletown and generally went there each summer. Summer always brought an exodus of upper-class New

be persuaded to come on for us, we shall expect her with brother, and we hope to see Sister too, and then if the hair which we sent, does not please Mama, she can find something here; if she is frightened at its being frizzed and curled, that can be combed out and she can cut it as she pleases, we could not get the barber to make any thing plainer, but I hope that nor any thing else will prevent her coming, it will make us so happy; and then we shall meet Papa at Hartford, and have the pleasure of being all together, where we were last separated. I am very glad that our dear Parents had a pleasant visit at New London, and dare say our friends there were happy to see you. I think Papa must by this time have received letters from Uncle John, or at least have heard from him, as Mr Watson told us he had received a letter from him, and some ornaments committed to his care for Brother. I have not yet purchased my piano, but have looked for it, and imagine I shall get one in a few days of my music master, I have mentioned to Brother that I wished the money sent on soon, that I might be able to pay for it directly, when I found one to please me, and send it on, so that I might find it at Lebanon. We last night went to the play, it was for the benefit of Mr Hewitt my music master, and as he is so attentive, I thought I could

---

Yorkers, some of whom owned second homes in the Manhattan countryside or farther away in Long Island, New Jersey, or (more recently) in Connecticut. Isaac Brunson, for instance, had a place in Greenfield Hill, Conn. which he bought from Timothy Dwight when the latter became president of Yale in 1795. New York newspapers more and more frequently carried advertisements of Connecticut houses for sale that were suitable for summer residence.

do no less than add my mite.[4] Sally Colt came over from New Ark one day this week, and returned the next, she is very much pleased with her visit there, but wishes to go home, and I believe expects to soon. We see Uncle Backus once in a while he is very well: our dancing school finishes this week, and we go to drawing between five & six in the morning, which makes us rise early; we have a great deal of exercise, and are very well. Mr Winthrop told Maria that Major Alden[5] had been in town, that he was very well, and wished to see us, but staid here so little while and was so busy that he could not call. Our best love attends our dear Parents and friends, and kind regards to all neighbors, your dutiful and affectionate Daughter

HARRIET TRUMBULL

4. The theater season always came to a close with a series of benefit performances for the members of the company. Mr. Hewitt's benefit on May 6 opened with a new medley overture composed by him, and the orchestra later played the overture to *Iphigenia* by Gluck. The program included a comedy, *Everyone has his Faults*, and a comic opera, *The Cottagers*, with music composed by Mr. Hewitt; and then, said the advertisements, "Mrs. Melmoth will speak an Address, called, the PORTRAIT PAINTER in which she will sketch the following characters, a Beaux; Belle; Real fine Lady; Miser; Epicure; Successful and Unsuccessful Speculator; Jack and Poll and Mrs. Melmoth." The evening concluded with "the celebrated, grand, serio, comic, military Pantomime," *Le Deserteur de Naples*, which had been "performed in the theaters of London upwards of 200 nights, with the most unbounded applause." The piece was interspersed with songs and choruses using "the original French Music composed by Monsigny and Phillidor"; and in Act I, M. Laurence danced a *pas de deux* with another gentleman "being his first appearance on any stage." *Mercantile Advertiser*, May 6.

5. Roger Alden, brigade major under General Jedediah Huntington during the Revolution, moved from Lebanon to Pennsylvania about 1790–1791.

*To Lydia Backus at Norwich*

New York [*Tuesday*] 19th May 1801

My Dear Cousin

We had the pleasure of receiving your letter on Sunday, and this morning Maria has been out to execute your commission, and I hope has done it in a manner that will please you, the bonnet is the newest fashion that has arrived, we think it pretty, and our only fear is that you may think it too small, it is intended doubtless for a dress bonnet, and in that case with the hair curled, I imagine, you will find it large enough, the whole of it, with the box, and ribbon, which Maria thought you might wish for, cost three, dollars, and four shillings, Connecticut currency; we will send it to Mr Lanmans care, to forward it to Norwich, and I hope it will reach you safe, soon, and be agreeable.

I am sorry your visit to Mama was interrupted, you must finish it after our return; which I expect will be very soon now, Mr Wadsworth is to come for us next week, and we shall be very happy to leave the noise and gaity of New York, for the society of our friends, and the still domestic pleasures that Lebanon affords. Maria desires her love to you and Julia,[1] in which she is join'd by your affectionate Cousin

Harriet Trumbull

Pray dear Cousin excuse the shortness of this, as our time here is very short we are full of business.

1. Sister of Lydia Backus.

*To Mrs. Trumbull at Hartford*

New York [*Wednesday*] May 20th 1801

MY DEAR MAMA

Saturday we spent the day at Mrs Fays with Mrs Phelps who is a great deal better and expects to go to Hartford very soon. Sister desired us to write very particularly about her—as she felt anxious to hear—she seems to be in very good spirits and looks well, tho she coughs a great deal—she is however much better than when she came from New Haven[1]—we called upon young Mrs Watson[2]—who is one of the sweetest women in the world—I already love her very much indeed, she seems so amiable and good—sunday morning I went to the Roman Catholic church with Mr and Miss Watkinson[3] and Mr Phillips—we then went with Harry to se Mrs and Miss Watson—and dined as usual at Mr Sebors. After Church we went to walk a little way upon the Battery and spent the evening at Mr Fitches—monday morning we went to call on Mrs Fairly[4] Mrs Brunson, Mrs Watson &c, and dined and spent the remainder of the day and evening at Mrs Sebors—tuesday morning we were up at five oclock to go to drawing school—I was out a shopping all the morning getting Lydia Backus's

1. Mrs. Phelps died within a year, and after the death of Mr. Phelps (1812), Faith and Daniel Wadsworth adopted their eldest daughter.

2. Eben Watson married Frances Sedgwick, daughter of Theodore Sedgwick of Massachusetts (Speaker of the House of Representatives), on April 9.

3. Undoubtedly two of the twelve children of Samuel Watkinson who emigrated from England to Middletown, Conn. in 1795. The sons received commercial training and experience in the New York firms of Samuel Corp, Moses Rogers, and William Woolsey and then went into business on their own in Hartford and New York.

4. The wife of James Fairlie who was at this time clerk of the New York Supreme Court. [41 Cortlandt St.]

bonnet and some things to carry home—we drank tea at Mrs Hopkins after which we called at Mrs Watsons and Mr Fitches—this morning we have been out makeing a multitude of calls—at Miss Murrays—Mrs Fays Mrs Sebors Miss Remsens[5] Mr Watsons Mr Coits and Mr Woolsey's, and Mr Atkinsons—we find as the time approches for our return our *business calls* &c begin to multiply and we have very little time to spare—I am indeed very very glad that Brother is coming so soon—we do really long to get home and shall leave New York and *most* of its inhabitants with *very little* regret, none I think with *less* than the family we live in—they are the least amiable and of course we feel less sorrow at parting from them—I suppose Lady Kitty will be married in a little while and I sincerely hope they will all be happy, she is a fine sensible well informed woman—but has I think lived too much in the *fashionable world* to have much of a *heart*—she has always treated us with extreme politeness but no affection—tho we have often felt *affectionately disposed towards her*—as to the younger branches of the family we have no great reason to love any of them—they possess no qualities which can render them very *engageing*—I think William the eldest is better by far than any of the rest—tho he is amazingly passionate yet I think he affects it half, and he is sometimes so *amaiable and obligeing and pretty* that you cant help loving him[6]—we have got so much used to drawing that I

5. Kitty and Jane, the 15-and 17-year-old daughters of John and Dorothy Remsen, are mentioned in Harriet Trumbull's later letters. [38 Pearl St.]

6. William Duer later became a judge on the New York Supreme Court and president of Columbia College.

hope we shall be able to do a good deal of it at home
and Harriet seems of late more encouraged about her music
and I dare say will take a great deal of pleasure in practicing
at home upon a good instrument—we do long to se you all
very much indeed and shall be rejoiced to se our dear
Brother very soon—I suppose this is one of the last letters
you will recieve from us—and we shall be heartily glad to
get out of this great *hen coop* of a city into dear old Hartford and Lebanon where our friends will be happy to see
us—adieu my dear dear Mama—give my best love to all
friends Papa Brother and Sister in particular and believe me
to be your very dutifull and affectionate Child

MARIA TRUMBULL

Harriets best love to all

# INDEX

*Abaellino, the Great Bandit,* 147*n*
*Abbé de l'Epée,* 41–42, 147*n*
Actors, 43, 110, 147*n*
Actresses, 42, 110, 173*n*
Adams, Abigail (Smith), 29, 128
Adams, John, 27
African Theatre, 132
Alden, Roger, 173 and *n*
Alexander, James, 13
Alexander, Sarah (Livingston), "Lady Stirling," 52, 84, 89, 156
Alexander, William, "Lord Stirling," 9, 13, 67*n*
Alexander family, 66*n*
Anglicanism, 28
Anna, Miss, 106
Anodine balsam, 50
Art. *See* Drawing lessons
Atkinson, Eliza, 98, 102
Atkinson, Elizabeth (Storer), 102, 109, 113, 132, 176
Atkinson, John, 102*n*
Atkinson, Mary Ann, 102
Austin, Mary, 97
Austin, Nancy, 97

Backus, Abigail (Trumbull), 8
Backus, Christopher: description of, 61, 82, 131, 148–49; requests money, 61*n*; mentioned, 74–173 *passim*
Backus, Ebenezer (b. 1712), 7, 8
Backus, Ebenezer (b. 1747), 80*n*
Backus, Eunice (Dyer), 7
Backus, Eunice (of Norwich), 122*n*
Backus, Julia, 174
Backus, Lydia, 80, 174
Backus family, 7
Baked beans, 88, 144
Balls, 85, 99, 124, 128, 155
Baltimore, Md., 153*n*
Barclay, Maria, 128
Barclay, Susan, 128
Barclay, Thomas, 128*n*
Battery, The, 34, 124, 132, 175
Benson, Catharine (Van Borsum), 71, 94, 98, 102
Benson, Robert, 92, 94, 98
Betsy, 96, 122
Bible, 84, 89
Blair, Hugh, Dr., 83*n*
Bleeker, Miss, 98
Bleeker, Elizabeth, 82*n*
Bloomingdale Rd., 156*n*
Bonnets, 73, 148, 153, 158, 174

Books: history, 52, 63, 133; geography, 63, 89; sermons, 83; novels, 83, 159. *See also* Bible
Boston Post Road, 156*n*
Boston Tea Party, 109*n*
Boudinot, Catherine, 164
Boudinot, Elias, 11
Boudinot, Elisha, 164
Bradley, Mrs. (Walter?), 77, 97, 129, 151–52*n*
Bridgeport, Conn., 89*n*
Broadway, 30, 31–34
Bronson, Anna (Olcott): birth of son, 97; mentioned, 109, 132, 151, 153, 165, 175
Bronson, Isaac, 89, 90, 92, 108, 172*n*
Broome, Henrietta, 72, 77, 151, 153
Broome, Samuel, 72*n*
Brown, Ann: oddity of, 66*n*–67*n*, 84, 90; social connections of, 66*n*; mentioned, 60, 147, 160
Brown, Betty, 134
Brown, Jesse, Jr., 59, 123*n*
Brown, Sarah, 66*n*
Brown, William Burnet, 66*n*
Browne, Mary (Burnet), 66*n*
Browne, Mary (French), 66*n*
Browne, William, 66*n*
Browne family, 66*n*
Brunson, Isaac. *See* Bronson, Isaac
Burnet, Mary (Van Horne), 66*n*
Burnet, William, 66*n*
Burr, Aaron, 25, 68, 73, 132
Business: crash of 1792, 14–15; partnerships, 20, 21; interstate, 21. *See also* Merchants
Butler, Justus, 49
Butter, 63, 96

Calico, 73, 76, 146
Cap crown, 80, 170
Cane (Caine), Mr. *See* Kane duels
Card playing, 85, 92–94, 108, 119
Card tables, 92
"Carlton House set," 53*n*
Carriages, 71, 72, 83, 90, 92, 114, 120, 128, 140, 143. *See also* Riding
Carter, Judith Walker, 67*n*
*Castle of Andalusia, The*, 128*n*
*Catherine and Petruchio*, 57*n*
Charity, 131, 132
Chauncy, Elihu, 24
Cheese, 116
Chicken pox, 115, 127
Children: education of, 2–3; visiting of, 3–4; in Trumbull household, 96*n*, 122*n*
*Children of the Abbey*, 159
China, 87*n*, 89*n*, 106*n*
Christmas, 75
Church, Angelica (Schuyler), 71, 72, 111, 124, 138, 145
Church, Elizabeth, 100, 124, 128, 138, 145
Church, John Barker, 38, 53, 75, 144*n*
Churches: in Conn., 28; in N.Y., 28–29, 32, 65, 108–09; on holidays, 75, 78. *See also* St. Paul's; St. Peter's; Trinity
Church family, 53*n*, 56, 100
Cigars, 43, 125
Cities, 39
City Hotel. *See* Tontine City Hotel
Clarke, Thaddeus, Dr., 88, 122, 135, 169
Clarkson family, 66*n*
Class consciousness. *See* Social class; Social distinctions
Coit, Levi, 59*n*, 114*n*, 176
Coit, Lydia (Howland), 59, 72, 75, 81, 109–27 *passim*, 153–54
Colt, Mary, 158, 159
Colt, Roswell, 62, 73–83 *passim*, 97–110 *passim*, 120, 125, 148–56 *passim*, 165

Colt, Sarah ("Sally"), 105, 129, 147–64 *passim*, 173
Columbian Academy of Painting, 36, 58*n*
Columbian Anacreontic Society. *See* Concert
Commerce (a game), 92
Concert, of Columbian Anacreontic Society, 81, 82*n*, 84, 99*n*
Congregationalists, 27–28
Connecticut: relations with N.Y., 2, 3, 4, 19–22; prejudices in, 3, 35–36, 37–40, 42, 43–44; opinion of New York in, 8, 44, 132, 133, 155, 177; and election of 1801, 23–27; religion in, 27–28; duel in, 126. *See also* Merchants
*Connecticut Courant*, 109*n*
Corp, Ann (Crammond), 71, 78, 120
Corp, Samuel, 71, 120, 175*n*
*Cottagers, The*, 173*n*
Cowles, Julia, 52*n*
Cumming, Mr., 97
Currant jelly, 136

Daggett, David, 25*n*
Dancers, 41, 110*n*, 173*n*
Dancing lessons: in Conn. 35–36; in N.Y., 36, 37, 99, 102, 138
Dancing masters, 36, 102*n*, 155*n*
Delacroix, Joseph, 132*n*
Democrats, 24, 68, 136*n*, 143. *See also* Republicans
Dennie, Joseph, 91*n*
*Deserteur de Naples, Le*, 40–41, 173*n*
Devero, John C., 36
Dinner, time of, 56, 92, 97, 110
Dramatics. *See* Theater; Actors; Actresses
Drawing lessons: in Conn., 35; in N.Y., 36–37, 129, 138, 173
Dresses, 51, 73, 76, 116, 166
Drinking, 24, 94, 133
Duels, 126, 144, 149
Duer, Alexander, 16, 51*n*
Duer, Catherine (Alexander), "Lady Kitty": background of, 9, 13–16, 66*n*; reputed poverty of, 9, 16, 31, 86–116; children of, 16, 51, 52, 176; appraisals of, 51, 70, 111, 168, 176; social engagements of, 81, 83, 95, 98, 103, 111, 143, 151; charges for board and room, 103, 145; smokes cigars, 125; will marry soon, 176; mentioned, 53, 60, 62, 67, 90, 106, 115, 152, 170. *See also* Duer household
Duer, Catherine, 16, 51*n*
Duer, Frances ("Fanny"), 16, 51, 81, 128*n*
Duer, Henrietta ("Harriet"), 16, 51, 128*n*
Duer, John: recommends new paper, 90; swearing of, 111–12; defends dueling, 126; mentioned, 16, 51, 81, 85, 124
Duer, Maria, 16, 51
Duer, Sarah ("Sally"), 16, 51, 72, 81
Duer, William, 9, 14–15
Duer, William Alexander: sleeps late, 90; swearing of, 111; defends dueling, 126; is passionate, 176; mentioned, 16, 51, 85, 124
Duer household: rooms, 51; furniture, 52; books, 52, 63, 133; heating, 52, 86; dinner, 51, 65, 67; breakfast, 63, 89, 166; is slovenly, 166–67
Dunlap, Elizabeth (Woolsey), 119*n*
Dunlap, William, 40, 41, 42, 147*n*
Dutton, Abigail (Backus), 73
Dutton, Hubbard, 73*n*
Dutton, Warren, 25*n*
Dwight, Mary (Woolsey), 120*n*

Dwight, Theodore, 25*n*
Dwight, Timothy, Rev., 25*n*, 26–27, 78*n*, 172*n*

Eclipse, of moon, 155
Edmund, 88, 96
Education: of children, 2–3; of girls, 13, 16, 34–39; English influence on, 38–39
Elderkin, Harriet, 154
Elderkin, Jedediah, 154*n*
Election of 1801: propaganda, 23–27; fear of violence, 24, 129, 136 and *n*; celebration, 124, 131. *See also* Inauguration, celebration of
Elliott, Benjamin, 70
Ellsworth, Oliver, 13*n*, 160*n*
Ely, Mary ("Polly"), 134
Ely, Zebulon, Rev., 28, 134*n*, 169
England, 19, 38–39, 154
*Everyone Has His Faults*, 173*n*

Fairlie, Mrs. James, 175
Falconi, M., 153*n*
Fashion: servility to, 37, 88; in dresses, 51, 73, 100, 146; in bonnets, 73, 148, 158, 174; of ladies smoking, 125; independence of, 39, 140; in wigs, 168
Fay, Elizabeth (Broome), mentioned, 63, 77, 89, 97, 128, 131, 151, 152, 153, 175, 176
Fay, Joseph, 68, 71
Federalists, 23–27, 68*n*, 136*n*
Figs, 162
Fire engines, 63*n*, 115*n*
Fires: of 1776, 31–32; of 1801, 61–65 *passim*, 115, 160
Fireworks, 132 and *n*
Fisk, John B., 111
Fitch, Miss, 147, 151
Fitch, William, 147*n*, 175, 176
Food: at parties, 81, 98, 102; at Lady Kitty's, 51, 63, 67
*Force of Calumny, The*, 110
"Fourteen mile round," 156*n*
Fox, Mary, 106, 134
France, 19, 34, 87*n*
Freemans meeting, 154

Games, 77. *See also* Card playing
Gautier, Mr., 97
Genesee Country: Wadsworth lands in, 103*n*; Morris lands in, 144*n*
Gig, 156
Giles, Aquila, 99
Gillet, Mr., 107*n*
Gingerbread, 87
Glover, Daniel, 114*n*
Glover, John I., 109, 113, 166
Glover, Thomas, 114
Goodwin, George, 109*n*
Gore, Christopher, 87*n*
Governors Island, 132*n*
Gracie, Archibald, 98
Gracie, Esther (Rogers), 98
Greenfield Hill, Conn., 172*n*
Guadaloupe, 19
Guthrie, William, 63, 89

Hairdressing, 84, 106, 158, 168, 172
Hamilton, Alexander, 13, 75, 102*n*
Hamilton, Elizabeth (Schuyler), 71, 72
Hampstead, England, 87
Handkerchiefs, 51
Hart, Miss, 156
Hartford, Conn.: builds theater, 40; compared with Lebanon, 58, 64, 80, 118, 156–57; fire at, 160; Trumbulls buy house in, 163
Hewitt, James: composes music, 57*n*, 116*n*, 138, 145, 173*n*; runs music business, 99, 116, 172;

gives lessons, 99, 111, 116, 138, 168
Hillhouse, James, 136*n*
Hobart, James Sloss, 119
Hoebuck, N. J., 144*n*
*Honest Thieves, The*, 153*n*
Hopkins, Lemuel, Dr., 25*n*, 50, 56*n*, 165*n*
Hopkins, Rebecca: marriage of, 97*n*; death of father, 165 and *n*; mentioned, 129, 151–64 *passim*
Hopkins, Samuel Miles, 119
Hopkins, Sarah (Rogers), 119, 128, 176
Howe, Sir William, 67*n*
Howland, Elizabeth Burt, 59, 81, 99, 114, 123
Howland, Joseph, 59*n*, 123, 127
Howland, Joseph, Jr., 59*n*, 101
Howland, Lydia (Bill), 124, 127, 140, 159
Hudson, Barzillai, 109*n*
Hudson, Henry, 44, 80–175 *passim*
Hume, David, 63, 133
Huntington, Jedediah, 100, 171, 173*n*
Huntington, Joshua, 121*n*, 122
Hyde, Abigail: identified, 64; is old maid, 67; knew James T. Watson, 71; makes sausages, 78; crown cap for, 80, 170; makes butter, 96; makes cake, 134
Hyde, Ebenezer, 106*n*
Hyde, Elizabeth, 106
Hyde, Eunice, 106
Hyde, Lucy (Huntington), 106
Hypochondria, 8, 49*n*

Inauguration, celebration of, 24, 132–33, 137, 143
India, 87*n*, 89*n*
*Invisible woman*, 152–53*n*
*Iphigenia* (Gluck's), 173*n*
Ivers, Boquet, 108, 151
Ivers, Eliza, 108, 151
Ivers, Hezekiah Beach, 151*n*

Jacob, 70
Jacobins, 23
Jay, John, 60*n*
Jay, Sarah (Livingston), 84*n*
Jay Commission, 60*n*, 87*n*
Jefferson, Joseph, 147*n*
Jefferson, Thomas, 68, 73, 132
Johnson, Mrs., 132

Kane, Elias, 144*n*
Kane, John, 144*n*
Kane, Oliver, 144 and *n*, 149
Kane duels, 126, 144, 149
Kinsey, Miss, 97
Kissam, Mr., 98
Kitty, "Lady." *See* Duer, Catherine (Alexander)
*Knights of Guadalquiver, The*, 57*n*
Kotzebue, August von, 110*n*, 153*n*
Kratter, Fritz, 147*n*

Lalliet, M. (dancing master), 102*n*, 155*n*
Lambert, Miss, 98
Lambert, Mr., 98
Lambert, Susannah (Rogers), 98*n*
Lanman, Peter, 74*n*
Lanman, Peter, Jr.: and marriage of John Trumbull, 86; marriage of, 88*n*, 101; visits Lebanon, 101, 118, 171, 174; mentioned, 60, 74, 81, 123
Laurence, M. (dancer), 41, 110*n*, 173*n*
Lauzun, Armand Louis de Gontaut, Duc de, 4
Lawrence, Messrs., 98
*Learned pig*, 152
Lebanon: description of, 4–6,

155; social life in, 6, 7, 64, 169; compared with N.Y., 10, 73, 155; compared with Hartford, 58, 64, 80, 118, 156–57
Leeds, England, 113*n*, 114*n*
Leffingwell, Fanny, 164, 166
Leffingwell, Sally Maria (Beers), 59, 151, 153, 156
Leffingwell, William, 59*n*, 87*n*, 129
*Liberty* (ship), 154*n*
Libraries, 52, 72, 159
Lieu table, 93
Lindley, Mr., (brother of Mrs. Murray), 143
Lindley, Susannah (Lownes), 143
Linn (Lynd), William, Rev., Abigail Adams on, 29
Little, Agnes (Stanton), 60, 74, 100, 102
Little, Jonathan, 56, 74, 100, 153
Liverpool, 154*n*
Livingston, Cornelia (Van Horne), 95
Livingston, Mrs. Peter, 75
Livingston, Philip, 95*n*, 98
Livingston, William, 66*n*
Livingston family, 66*n*
London, 154*n*
Lotteries, 162*n*
Lyman, Lydia, 135
Lyman, Mary (Barker), 135
Lyman, William, 135

Maclay, William, 12
McClellan, Faith (Williams), 164*n*
McClellan, John, 164*n*
McCracken, John, 97, 101, 102
McCurdy, John, 122
Manhattan Water Company, 53*n*
Manners, 12, 16, 36, 37
Mantuamaker, 52, 99
Marriage: interstate, 20–21; age of men at, 87*n*, 88*n*, 95*n*, 128*n*
Melmoth, Mrs. (actress), 173*n*
Merchants: and Anglicanism, 28; difficulties in Conn., 18–19; emigrate to N.Y., 19–20, 49*n*–175*n passim*
*Mercury and New England Palladium*, 25*n*
Middletown, Conn., 171
Ministers: of Conn., 26–27, 28; of N.Y., 29, 90
Mobs, 124
Morgan, John: bought earrings, 106; sold house, 161, 162; mentioned, 18, 85, 89, 97, 101, 168, 170, 171
Morgan, Sally (Lancelot), 142, 160, 163, 171
Morgan, Weltha: social engagements of, 59, 97, 114, 121, 127, 151, 153, 154; lives at Glovers, 113, 166; marriage of, 114*n*; goes to drawing school, 121, 127–28; mentioned, 56, 81, 86, 106, 108, 129, 171
Morris, Robert, 144*n*
Morris, Thomas, 144*n*
Morse, Jedidiah, 25*n*
Muirson, George, Jr., Dr., 120*n*
Mumford, Benjamin M., 128, 133, 155–56
Murray, Hannah: accomplishments of, 111; 114; mentioned, 103, 108, 113, 128–44 *passim*, 156, 176
Murray, Hannah (Lindley), 111 and *n*, 143
Murray, John, 103, 111, 143
Murray, Mary: accomplishments of, 111, 114; mentioned, 103, 108, 113, 128–44 *passim*, 156, 176
Murray family: act like Conn.

people, 114; ball of, 128, hospitality of, 143–44
Music: lessons in Conn., 35; lessons in N.Y., 36–37; method of teaching, 138; composers of, 173*n*. *See also* Hewitt, James; Singing
Muslin, 51, 166

Neilson (Nielson, Nelson), William, 16
Nelson balls, 105 and *n*
Nelson, Horatio, 105*n*
Newark, N.J., 163, 164*n*, 173
New City Tavern. *See* Tontine City Hotel
New Haven, Conn., 35, 49, 175
New Jersey, 66*n*
New London, Conn., 19, 28, 172
New Orleans, La., 114*n*
New York: relation with Conn., 2, 3, 4, 19–22; Conn. opinions of, 8, 44, 132, 133, 155, 177; in 1789, 9–10; crash of 1792, 14–15; social life in, 17; description of, 30–34; occupation by British, 34, 67*n*; noise of, 33, 44. *See also* Merchants
New-York Academy of Fine Arts, 36
Norwich, Conn., 5, 7, 19, 28
Nova Scotia, 128*n*

O'Keefe, John, 128*n*
Oldschool, Oliver, 91*n*
Oysters, 49, 98
*Orion* (ship), 63*n*

Park Theater. *See* Theater
Patterson, John W., 148, 151
Pearl earrings, 106
Pell, Miss, 127–28, 140, 143, 154
Persians, 100, 116
*Peru Revenged, or the Death of Pizarro*, 40, 153*n*
Petticoats, 51
Phelps, Jennet (Broome), 72*n*, 174
Phelps, Timothy, 60, 62, 72, 97, 175*n*
Philadelphia, Pa., 13, 24, 89*n*, 143*n*
*Philadelphia* (U.S. frigate), 19
Philipsburg, 123*n*
Philipse Manor, 123*n*
Phillips, George, 114*n*
Phillips, George Thompson, 114, 125, 162, 175
Piano, purchase of, 60, 99, 162, 172
Pickering, Timothy, 102, 121, 165
Pierce, Dr., 171
Pierpont, Hezekiah Beers, 86, 88*n*
Pipes, 125
*Pizarro in Peru*, 153*n*
Plays. *See* Theater
Pomeroy, Miss, 127
*Pope Joan* (a game), 85
*Portfolio, The*, 91*n*, 121
Powell, Mrs. (actress), 42
Preaching, 29
Prices: of hairdressing, 84; of sugar plumbs, 105, 162; of pearl earrings, 106; of board and room, 145; of calico, 146; of bonnets, 148, 158, 174; of muslin, 166; of wigs, 168

Quakers, 6, 143

Ray, Mr. and Mrs. Cornelius, 98
Reading. *See* Books; Bible
Religion: and Backus family, 7; and Trumbull family, 7, 27–30; in N.Y., 8, 90; and politics, 23, 26–27, 30*n*; in Conn., 27–28; and social class, 30*n*
Remsen, Jane, 176

Remsen, Mr. and Mrs. John, 176*n*
Remsen, Kitty, 176
"Republican court", 9–11
Republicans: immorality of, 23–24; in Conn., 25; propaganda of, 26–27; religion of, 30*n*; fear Federalist conspiracy, 136*n*
Riding, 66, 81, 89, 120, 156. *See also* Carriages
Robertson, Alexander, 58*n*
Robertson, Archibald, 58*n*
Robespierre, Maximilien Francois Marie Isidore de, 87*n*
Robinson, Ichabod, 122, 134
Robinson, Beverly, 128
Robinson, Lydia, 56, 122
Robinson, Morris, 128*n*
Roche, Regina Maria, 159*n*
Rodgers, John, Rev., 29*n*
Rogers, Miss, 98 and *n*
Rogers, Henry, 98*n*
Rogers, Moses, 98*n*, 119, 175*n*
Rogers, Nehemiah, 98*n*
Rogers, Sarah (Woolsey), 119
Rollin, Charles, 52
Rome, N.Y., 150
Rutherfurd, Walter, 75, 77

St. Paul's, 29, 32, 71, 89
St. Peter's, 114, 175
Salem, Mass., 66*n*
Sanford, Peleg, 143
Sarah, "Aunt," 134, 144
Sausages, 78
Sebor, Eliza, 44, 114, 118, 120, 171
Sebor, Elizabeth (Winthrop): fears Republican disturbances, 137; mentioned 63–175 *passim*. *See also* Sebor family
Sebor, Jacob: transmits money, 88, 116, 129, 137; mentioned, 63–175 *passim*. *See also* Sebor family
Sebor family, cordiality of, 65, 72, 148, 171
Sedgwick, Theodore, 175*n*
Sermons, 29, 63, 83, 109
Servants, 94, 120
Shad, 167
Shopping, 170. *See also* Fashion; Prices
Sightseeing, 152
Silk, 51
Silliman, Benjamin, 42, 43–44, 45, 110*n*
Silliman, Maria (Trumbull), 54*n*
Simon, 88, 96
Sinclair, Sir John, 78
Singing: of young people, 35, 37, 114; professional, 41, 57*n*, 173*n*; at parties, 94, 97; lessons in, 138
Sleighing, 120
Smallpox, 4, 120*n*
Smoking, 43, 125
Social behavior: in Lebanon, 6, 169; of Trumbulls, 6–7, 11; in New England, 12–13; in N.Y., 17, 114, 166
Social class, and religion, 30*n*
Social distinctions, 10–11, 14, 87–88
Social sensitivity: of J. Trumbull, 11–12; of William Maclay, 12; of Trumbull girls, 18, 121, 138, 140, 142, 147–48, 168–69
Society, intercolonial connections of upper class, 66*n*
Southworth, Betty, 73, 107, 134, 169, 170
*Spanish Castle, The*, 57*n*
*Spectator, The*, 36–39
Spencer (jacket), 83
Spinsters, 67
Spoliations, 19
Stagecoach, 21, 101, 161
Stevens, Ebenezer, 109, 148, 151
Stevens, Rebecca, 109*n*, 113
Stewart, Jane (Winthrop), 109, 113, 128, 137*n*

Stewart, William, 113*n*
Stiles, Ezra, Rev., 28
Stirling, "Lady." *See* Alexander, Sarah (Livingston)
Stirling, "Lord." *See* Alexander, William
Storm of Dec. 12, 62*n*
Storer, Miss, 102
Stratford, Conn., 51
Strong, Nathan, Rev., 160*n*
Sugar plumbs, 105, 162
Summer homes, 143–44, 172*n*
Swearing, 111
Sylvia, 96 and *n*, 122*n*

Taintor, John, 168
Taylor, Miss, 114
Terry, Catherine (Wadsworth), 129*n*, 158*n*
Terry, Nathaniel, 129, 160*n*
Theater: Conn. prejudice against, 39–44 *passim*, 110*n*; scenery in, 40–41; repertoire of, 41–42, 57*n*, 110*n*, 128*n*, 147*n*, 153*n*, 173*n*; reviews, 41–42, 147*n*; offends N.Y. ladies, 42–43; morality of, 43–44, 110*n*; African, 132. *See also* Actors; Actresses
Thies, Mr., 154
Thomas, 64
Tiffany, Mr., 70
Tisdale, Mrs., 107
Tom, 122
*Tom Come Tickle Me* (a game), 77
*Tom Thumb*, 110 and *n*
Tontine City Hotel, 81, 82*n*, 155
Trade. *See* Merchants
Trapp, Hannah, 134
Trinity Church, 32, 71, 72, 89
Trumbull, Abigail, 69, 73, 78, 101*n*
Trumbull, David, 69*n*, 131
Trumbull, Eunice (Backus): family background of, 7; ill health of, 8; dislikes theater, 39, 146–47; mentioned, 49–176 *passim*. *See also* Trumbull family
Trumbull, Faith (Robinson), 122*n*
Trumbull, John (artist): on fashionable education, 38, 60*n*; and John B. Church, 54*n*; marriage of, 78, 86–87; mentioned, 84*n*, 95, 103*n*, 145, 172
Trumbull, John (poet-lawyer), 25*n*
Trumbull, John M., 101
Trumbull, Jonathan, 7, 9, 28, 122*n*
Trumbull, Jonathan, Jr.: family background of, 6, 7; character of, 6–7, 11, 27; career of, 8–9, 10, 13, 23, 27; receives letter from Sir John Sinclair, 78; picture of, 84; visits New London, 172; mentioned, 49–176 *passim*. *See also* Trumbull family
Trumbull, Jonathan George Washington, 135
Trumbull, Joseph (1737–1778), 9
Trumbull, Joseph (1782–1861), 134
Trumbull, Sarah ("Sally"), 68, 69*n*, 70, 73, 79, 105
Trumbull, Sarah (Backus), 69*n*
Trumbull, Sarah Hope (Harvey), 38, 87*n*
Trumbull family: religious nature of, 7, 27–30; aversion to Church family, 38, 53–54, 100

Van Horne family, 66*n*
Van Wyke, Miss, 154
Varick, Maria (Roosevelt): hospitality of, 94, 98; mentioned, 71, 82, 93, 109
Varick, Richard: party of, 92–94, 98; mentioned, 71, 72, 75, 82, 113
Vauxhall Garden, 132

Ventriloquism, 151*n*
Vestris (ballet master), 41
*Virgin of the Sun, The*, 153*n*
Virginia, 10, 67*n*
Visiting, rationale of, 3–4, 12–13, 17

Wadsworth, Daniel: visits N.Y., 49, 54, 174; letters of, 49–50, 136; visits Lebanon, 127, 136; adopts child, 175*n*; mentioned, 24*n*, 58, 118
Wadsworth, Faith (Trumbull): in N.Y., 4; in Philadelphia, 13; mentioned, 35, 68, 118, 127
Wadsworth, Harriet, 158*n*
Wadsworth, James: identified, 103; duels of, 126, 133, 144, 149; at Murray ball, 128; mentioned, 124, 152, 160, 161
Wadsworth, Jeremiah, 13*n*, 103*n*, 160*n*
Wadsworth, Mrs. Jeremiah, 158*n*, 159
"Walpole paper," 90
Washington, George: J. Trumbull secretary to, 9; social standards of, 10, 11*n*; gave Lady Kitty in marriage, 14; friend of Ann Brown, 66*n*; letters to Sir John Sinclair, 78*n*
Washington, Martha (Dandridge), 66*n*
Washington, D.C., 137
Watkinson, Miss, 175
Watkinson, Mr., 175
Watkinson, Samuel, 175*n*
Watson, Ebenezer, 109, 125, 133, 153
Watson, Frances Pamela (Sedgwick), 175
Watson, Hannah (Bunce), 109*n*
Watson, James: helps relatives, 66*n*, 81*n*, 109*n*; disciplines coachman, 120; fears Republican disturbances, 133, 143; mentioned, 53–176 *passim*. *See also* Watson family
Watson, James Talcott, 71, 110, 111*n*
Watson, John, 66*n*
Watson, Maria, 66–175 *passim*. *See also* Watson family
Watson, Mary (Talcott), 66–175 *passim*. *See also* Watson family
Watson family: cordiality of, 72, 87, 96–97; Trumbull girls overnight with, 114, 120, 133, 143, 147; prejudiced against James Wadsworth, 133
Watts, Anne, 120, 121
Watts, Catherine, 120, 121
Watts, Mary (Alexander), 67, 71, 83, 140, 143, 147
Watts, Robert, 67*n*
Webster, Noah, Jr., 25*n*, 37
Wells, Miss (drawing teacher), 35
West Indies, 18–19, 41
*Who's the Dupe?*, 147*n*
Wigs, 158, 168, 172
Williams, Joseph, 59
Williams, Mary ("Polly"), 134
Williams, Mary (Trumbull), 70*n*
Williams, Nathan, 70
Williams, Sarah ("Sally"), 59
Williams, Solomon, 106
Williams, Thomas, Dr., 134*n*
Williams, William (1731–1811), 70
Williams, William (1777–1839), 106, 122, 134, 144
Williamson, Miss, 81
Windham, Conn., 7
Wine, 94, 124
Winthrop, Francis Bayard, 71, 137*n*, 173
Winthrop, Phoebe (Taylor), 71

*Wives as They Were, and Maids as They Are*, 128*n*
Wolcott, Frederick, 121*n*, 122
Wolcott, Oliver, 121–22
Woodstock, Conn., 164
Woodworth, Walter, 95
Woolsey, Abigail (Howland), 57, 58–59, 72, 75, 78, 81, 176
Woolsey, Anne (Muirson), 119
Woolsey, Elizabeth (Dwight), 119, 122, 127, 135
Woolsey, George Muirson, 59*n*, 119*n*
Woolsey, William Walton, 78*n*, 119, 156, 175*n*
Wortman, Tunis, 132 and *n*

Yale College, 26, 39, 101*n*, 134*n*
Yankee, 132
Yates, Margaret (Winthrop), 113*n*, 137
Yonkers, N.Y., 123*n*

*Colophon:* The type faces used in this book are Linotype Palatino for the text and Cooper Black italic for the display. The printing is from the type by Heritage Printers, Inc., on Warren's Olde Style antique wove paper. The book is bound in Columbia cloth and Elephant Hide paper, and was designed by Gary Gore.